CONTEMPORARY ART, SYSTEMS AND THE AESTHETICS OF DISPERSION

Using five case studies of contemporary art, this book uses ideas of systems and dispersion to understand identity and experience in late capitalism.

This book considers five artists who exemplify contemporary art practice: Seth Price; Liam Gillick; Martin Creed; Hito Steyerl; and Theaster Gates. Given the diversity of materials used in art today, once-traditional artistic mediums and practices have become obsolete in describing what artists do today. Francis Halsall argues that, in the face of this obsolescence, the ideas of system and dispersion become very useful in understanding contemporary art. That is, practitioners now can be seen to be using whatever systems of distribution and display are available to them as their creative mediums. The two central arguments are first that any understanding of what art is will always be underwritten by a related view of what a human being is; and second that these both have a particular character in late capitalism or, as is named here, the Age of Dispersion.

The book will be of interest to scholars and students working in art history, contemporary art, studio art, and theories of systems and networks.

Francis Halsall is Lecturer in the History and Theory of Modern and Contemporary Art at the National College of Art and Design, Ireland and Co-Director of Master Programs, Art in the Contemporary World.

Routledge Focus on Art History and Visual Studies

Routledge Focus on Art History and Visual Studies presents short-form books on varied topics within the fields of art history and visual studies.

World-Forming and Contemporary Art
Jessica Holtaway

The Power and Fluidity of Girlhood in Henry Darger's Art
Leisa Rundquist

Buckminster Fuller's World Game and Its Legacy
Timothy Stott

Post-Digital Letterpress Printing
Research, Education and Practice
Edited by Pedro Manuel Reis Amado, Ana Catarina Silva and Vítor Quelhas

Bodily Engagements with Film, Images, and Technology
Somavision
Max Ryynänen

Performance, Art and Politics in the African Diaspora
Necropolitics and the Black Body
Myron M. Beasley

For more information about this series, please visit: https://www.routledge.com/ Routledge-Focus-on-Art-History-and-Visual-Studies/book-series/FOCUSAH

Contemporary Art, Systems and the Aesthetics of Dispersion

Francis Halsall

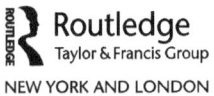
Routledge
Taylor & Francis Group

NEW YORK AND LONDON

First published 2023
by Routledge
605 Third Avenue, New York, NY 10158

and by Routledge
4 Park Square, Milton Park, Abingdon, Oxon, OX14 4RN

Routledge is an imprint of the Taylor & Francis Group, an informa business

ISBN: 9781032324920 (hbk)
ISBN: 9781032324937 (pbk)
ISBN: 9781003315322 (ebk)

DOI: 10.4324/9781003315322

Typeset in Times New Roman
by codeMantra

Contents

Figures

Acknowledgements

I am very grateful to Isabella Vitti at Routledge for all the help and support they gave. My colleagues Declan Long and Rachel O'Dwyer very generously responded to earlier drafts with really helpful observations. Several generations of students on the MA *Art in the Contemporary World* have had the patience to listen to the ideas take shape in several seminars. And of course, thanks to Isabel, the very best reader of my words and my mind.

Foreword

Francis Halsall

This book was written during remarkable circumstances when the word 'unprecedented' first became commonplace and then a fatigued cliché. Individually and collectively we've been forced to reconsider our relationships to space since February 2020 and the outbreak of Covid-19. There are no activities, no movements, occupations of public or even private spaces that we have been able to take for granted. Familiar sites such as pubs, shops, gyms, hairdressers, spaces of worship and living rooms were closed off to publics to varying degrees. In Ireland, 2 km; 5 km; 20 km; county boundaries; the island; Europe were just some of the zones temporarily employed as limits to movement.

Although this book was written in unprecedented circumstances, its subjects and arguments had already been mapped out and rehearsed in lectures, seminars and texts.[1] What was unexpected, however, was the emergence of two main and recurrent themes that inform the whole discussion. First is the importance (even if not acknowledged) of Robert Smithson for contemporary art practices. Through his exploration of systems, entropy, material and affect, he offered an alternative line of flight for art out of the twin dead ends of modernism: Greenbergian medium specificity and formalist abstraction; and anti-art, conceptualism and the linguistic turn associated with Marcel Duchamp. Second is the spectre of the End of Art which in this case implicates not only the dispersion and dissipation of art into wider systems of experience, commerce communication and control but also the horizon of human finitude when faced with both climate crisis and technological obsolesce. After all, as Niklas Luhmann said in his typically mordant manner: *This idea of humanism cannot continue. Who would seriously and deliberately want to maintain that society could be formed on the model of a human being, that is, with a head at the top and so on?*[2] I mention these themes now so as to acknowledge them but also to bracket them so that they don't dominate the following discussion; they are revisited in the final pages. There are two reasons for this. First, the book is, predominantly, a consideration, in the context of systems, of the dispersed conditions of subjectivity in late capitalism and how art might mimic those effects. It is not intended as a contribution to discussions in Art

History, and the examples here are very familiar and whilst I hope they will give something of the character of Contemporary Art to a general audience, they are not unpacked in a rigorous art historical way. Second, I am wary of adding to the ever-growing list of jeremiads about the end of art which are mostly delivered by middle-aged men mourning their faded youth in the guise of the critique that things are not as good as they used to be. I will not pound any more nails into the coffin of my youth.

There is very little, if anything, positive to be said about the conditions of living in the time of a pandemic. But two things did become apparent. First, it was rapidly demonstrated that we are all significantly, inextricably, unavoidably, connected together in a global system. A virus emerging at one particular place in the planet did, within a breathtakingly short time, affect everyone on that planet. The world system is a single entity. Within its circuits, various things including people, money, information, ideas and memes are transmitted. And viruses, too. Second, it also became clear that the solution to the problem was going to involve collective action not only in local communities or even nations but also across the whole planet as people cooperated in finding solutions such as vaccines and treatments. These two insights laced together by the themes of interconnection and collective action hint at what form a new type of politics, still only its nascent form, might take. This is a politics of improvisation involving collaborations not only between humans but also between other agents such as animals, objects, systems and environments.

We are all products of our environments, children of the systems we inhabit. To think in this way is to think phenomenologically. The philosophy of phenomenology considers how consciousness, bodies, technology and environments are profoundly inseparable. This means that minds are folded into the flesh of bodies and extended, via various limbs, appendages, prostheses and technologies into their environments. It is bodies and their contexts that think, and not just disembodied minds.

Different bodies allow for different types of thought. A skilled artisan, adept at working with certain materials, with a highly trained muscle memory must think very differently about their medium than someone who knows nothing about the processes involved. This is because their body behaves and feels and thinks in certain manners and has certain capacities and potentials. A potter evidently has a very different relationship to clay than a dancer. They might respond very differently to the sticky wet stuff because of how their bodies interact with it. For a dancer it is likely to simply be something that must be scraped of one's shoes, a component of the soil in their garden, whilst for a potter it is the origin of their craft.

As Maurice Merleau-Ponty put it in his book *Phenomenology of Perception*: 'Our own body… is in the world as the heart is in the organism; it keeps the visible spectacle constantly alive, it breathes life into it and sustains it inwardly, and with it forms a system.'[3]

In thinking about minds in such a manner, Merleau-Ponty recognised that all experiences and thoughts are part of larger systems. This means that, as a result of being a part of these systems, all experiences and thoughts are also a product of those systems. Another thinker about systems, Gregory Bateson, also thought about how minds are enmeshed into complex systems through being situated in particular zones. In *Steps to an Ecology of Mind*, he talks about minds that don't end at the edges of bodies. They are not bounded by the skin. Minds, he says, are a: 'network of pathways … not bounded with consciousness but extends to include the pathways of all unconscious mentation—both autonomic and repressed, neural and hormonal.'[4]

To put this another way, it is not just people that think but environments too. Systems, and the zones they occupy, create thought. Conceivably, then, particular zones promote particular ways of thinking. Maybe some environments are more creative than others, or more loving, or violent or addictive.

On the one hand, the local systems we inhabit are parts of a much bigger, single global system that's been called the World System (Jameson) or the Network Society (Castells). Here everything is globally connected in a system of exchange where information, money, products and bodies circulate. This is the zone of late capitalism, the information society and social media.

On the other hand, if it is whole systems that think, then those thoughts are not limited to the people who occupy environments but bleeds out into everything that they are made up from. Perhaps the World System itself is a mind in the sense that Bateson meant. It is an alien intelligence that has emerged amidst the networks of communication and control that have grown and spread, like viruses over the last 70 years. And if it is a *mind*, what is it thinking about? Does it care about us? Will it sleep? Can it dream? And what does it want? Hopefully the artists surveyed in this book give the beginnings of an answer to these seemingly impossible questions.

Notes

1 'Actor-Network Aesthetics: The Conceptual Rhymes of Bruno Latour and Contemporary Art,' in Muecke & Felski (eds.) *New Literary History*, Vol. 47, No. 2/3, Recomposing the Humanities—with Bruno Latour (SPRING & SUMMER 2016) pg. 439–461; 'Art as Systems Irritants: Liam Gillick's Use of Systems,' in Gosse & Stott (eds), *Nervous Systems: Art, Systems, and Politics since the 1960s* (Duke University Press, 2021).

2 Niklas Luhmann, *Social Systems*, trans. J. Bednarz Jr and D. Baeker (Stanford, CA: Stanford University Press, 1996) pg. 213.

3 Maurice Merleau-Ponty, *The Phenomenology of Perception*, trans. Colin Smith,(London: Routledge 2002)) pg. 235.

4 Gregory Bateson, *Steps to an Ecology of Mind* (Chicago, IL: University of Chicago Press, 1972) pg. 319.

References

Bateson, Gregory, *Steps to an Ecology of Mind*, Chicago, IL: University of Chicago Press, 1972

Halsall, Francis, 'Actor-Network Aesthetics: The Conceptual Rhymes of Bruno Latour and Contemporary Art', in Stephen Muecke & Rita Felski (eds.) *New Literary History*, Vol. 47, No. 2/3 (pp. 439–461), Recomposing the Humanities—with Bruno Latour, SPRING & SUMMER, 2016

Halsall, Francis, 'Art as Systems Irritants: Liam Gillick's Use of Systems', in Johanna Gosse & Tim Stott (eds.), *Nervous Systems: Art, Systems, and Politics since the 1960s* (pp. 173–191), Durham: Duke University Press, 2021

Luhmann, Niklas, *Social Systems*, trans. John Bednarz Jr and Dirk Baeker, Stanford, CA: Stanford University Press, 1996

Merleau-Ponty, Maurice, *The Phenomenology of Perception*, trans. Colin Smith, London: Routledge2002

Introduction
Systems Everywhere! The Age of Dispersion

This is a book about two intimately related things, which, I claim, are best considered systemic and dispersed. They are art and the humans that make it. It borrows its title from Seth Price's essay from 2002, 'Dispersion.' But where Price was primarily considering media and in particular the distribution of images across those media, I want to consider social systems more generally. My central claim is that both contemporary art and humans at present can be best understood, not as fixed and stable objects with immutable identities, but rather as instances of *dispersion* across systems of distribution, communication and control. In other words, we might best understand both works of art and the people that make and experience them, not by looking at individual objects or people, but rather at the systems that they are situated within. This argument is supported by the accompanying claim (laid out in Chapter 1) that any understanding of what art is will be underwritten by an understanding of what it means to be human. A model of art depends on a model of subjectivity, and this dependency pivots around the hinge of technology.

The starting point for Price's essay was Conceptual Art which he identifies as an expanded field of practices spanning the 20th century that originate with Duchamp and the Readymade. These include: the Linguistic Turn of the 1960s; Institutional Critique; and the relational and collaborative practices that appeared in the 1990s. The importance of Conceptual Art, Price claims, is that: 'one of the ways in which the Conceptual project in art has been most successful is in claiming new territory for practice.'[1] The new territory claimed by Conceptual Art is, Price identifies, a space of: 'commercial distribution, decentralization, and dispersion.'[2] By dispersion Price means that art within the historical and discursive horizon of Conceptualism (from the 1960s) is now understood as not occupying a single and unique position in time and space. Instead, a work of art has an identity that is articulated through the different mediums by which it might be experienced such as photographs, texts and facsimiles. Another way of thinking about this condition is that art is no longer confined by plinths, frames or galleries as privileged sites of display but can now be not only considered as dispersed across different systems but also that this dispersed condition is part of its primary subject matter.

DOI: 10.4324/9781003315322-1

Price establishes the horizon for the development of Conceptual Art in the 20th century as the profound societal shifts brought about by the twin factors of technological developments, such as computing and telecommunications and the economic shift to late capitalism. Both of these brought into being a new world order that is best understood as a global system that operates through a logic of networks and distribution which I refer to here as the *Age of Dispersion*. The *Age of Dispersion* emerges alongside both the communication and computing systems of the 20th century and discourses including Cybernetics and Systems Theory that are developed with those technologies to study those systems. The global system of the *Age of Dispersion* creates a shared horizon for what might otherwise be identified as a diverse range of practices. They are all self-reflexive in considering this horizon, which is to say that they have all made the economic, social and institutional conditions of their distribution and display their primary subject matter rather than experiments with representational, formal or aesthetic content.

In the chapters that follow, I consider five paradigmatic contemporary artists that both work with and exemplify the conditions of dispersion in systems: Seth Price; Liam Gillick; Martin Creed; Hito Steyerl; and Theaster Gates. These artists demonstrate the formal diversity of contemporary art in 2022 in which traditional artistic mediums and practices have been replaced with systemic process in which artists use whatever systems of distribution and display are available to them. My claim is that these systemic processes are underwritten by the contemporary conditions of subjectivity in *The Age of Dispersion*. That is, like art, human subjectivity is similarly dispersed across systems of distribution, communication and control.

However, if, through acts of dispersion, contemporary art might exemplify contemporary conditions of subjectivity, then this exemplification runs the risk of serving as mere passive reflection in lieu of critique. To phrase this as a rhetorical question: what ways can artists respond to accusation that in celebrating dispersion they are complicit in the logic of neo-liberal market fundamentalism? Art can, all too often, can seem to be the R&D Department for late capitalism exemplified by the accelerationist Pop Art of someone like KAWS (Brian Donnelly).[3] Contemporary artists face the challenge of how they can offer meaningful and effective critical engagement. Without this ability to facilitate critique, they risk appearing as mere compensatory or deflationary gestures in the face of the dispersion of subjectivity in contemporary society.

But whilst contemporary systems of dispersion feature in each of the examples I discuss, none of these artists merely accept or celebrate these conditions. Instead through techniques of abstraction, deflation or mischief, each artist offers aesthetic strategies for representing these systems and mimicking their functions whilst also offering the potential to disrupt them. Central to this disruption, I argue, are strategies of obfuscation, disappointment and misdirection.

Systems

Definitions of systems must, by necessity, be somewhat abstract as they can apply to a wide variety of instances. However, some basic principles can be identified. A system is a set of elements connected so they form a recognisable and coherent whole, and this connection performs some form of recognisable function. A system orders its world. Kenneth Boulding, the pioneer of *General Systems Theory* in the 20th century, called a system simply: 'anything that is not chaos. We could turn the pattern around and define a system as any structure that exhibits order and pattern.'[4] Systems reduce the complexity of their environments and by doing so become, somewhat, distinct from them. An ant colony, for example, just like a brain, is not reducible to its surroundings. They each have separate identities even if the physical borders are hard to discern. To understand a system means to understand what it does. An economic system, for example, reduces all of the messy complication of the world into the abstractions of financial transactions. Systems have functions, which are particular to themselves. The trick is in working out what, exactly, those functions might be.

If you look at the world through the lens of systems, you will find them everywhere. This is what the systems-theorist Stafford Beer meant when he said 'a system is not something given in nature';[5] that is, systems are defined and then observed by us as a result of our interactions with them. That said, people who think about systems tend to talk about them in one of two ways.

On the one hand, systems might be used as metaphors to describe and explain our complex world and the behaviours and patterns that seem to occur within it. Gamblers may have a system by which they imagine they can place winning bets. Ikea has a whole range of shelves, draws and cupboards that they describe as Storage Solution Systems on their website:

> IKEA storage systems are designed to help you keep all your things organised throughout your home. Each system has parts, such as shelves, frames and cabinets that you can put together in unique combinations to suit your space and needs.[6]

In his early March 2021 interview with Oprah Winfrey, about his relationship with the British Royal family, Prince Harry made the following observations: that his brother and father were

> trapped within the system' of the Royal Family; that it was 'really hard because I am part of the system with them, I always have been' and was 'very aware' that his brother Prince William 'can't leave that system but I have.

It seems that Harry is using the word system here in a metaphorical way to describe relations rather than physical infrastructure. He wasn't literally 'trapped' by being locked up but rather felt compelled to behave in certain ways because of the history of his family. In the same way, Ikea's shelves are not literally systems but rather collections of interlocking parts; they are not, in the formal vocabulary of Systems Theory 'Autopoietic,' that is dynamic and self-organising in the way an ant colony is.

In these cases, system explains how relationships, processes and patterns may appear to us. In other words, from these perspectives, systems do not name actually existing things and structures in the world but rather describe a way of looking at the world and understanding our relationship to it.

However, systems might be considered underlying structures in the world that serve particular functions. Meteorologists talk about weather systems; town planners devise transport systems; engineers might design systems in factories to process anything from food to motor cars. From this perspective, systems actually exist and we know this because we can see them, or at the very least parts of them, and what they do. Arguably the most important such system is the internet. If the internet is a system made of different component things, then, presumably, it's theoretically possible (even if practically impossible) to weigh it. It is not a metaphor, but a literal thing comprising myriad interconnected elements. From this perspective, systems are not defined by us but rather discovered and identified through our interactions with them.

We know the internet is a physical thing that performs functions because we can see the ecological impact of its underlying infrastructure.[7] The processors, networks and cables required for online connectivity use up vast amounts of natural resources including fossil fuels, water and precious metals. As a recent report into the carbon footprint of the internet put it: 'charging up a single tablet or smart phone requires a negligible amount of electricity;[but] using either to watch an hour of video weekly consumes annually more electricity in the remote networks than two new refrigerators use in a year.'[8]

The use of words like 'virtual' or 'cloud' suggests that the online world is abstract and disembodied. But as James Ball puts it in his book *The System*, about 'who owns the internet and how it owns us,' the internet is a physical thing made up of cables, mechanisms and huge data centres connected in a global system. All elements of this physical infrastructure are owned and managed accordingly and 'We refer to the online world as if it's abstract from the reality we all occupy every day: this is a myth, and it's a myth that obscures where the real power lies.'[9]

There are people implicated in all of this too. Each time content is moderated in social media what *Wired* calls a 'a vast, invisible pool of human labor' checks it and reports that already in 2014, there were over 100,000 people moderating content of world's social media sites, mobile apps and cloud storage services, which was around twice the amount of people working directly for Google and nearly 14 times that of Facebook.[10]

In both uses of system – as metaphor and infrastructure – there are two things at stake.

First is how useful it is to describe our contemporary world. A system is a set of elements connected so they form a recognisable and coherent whole, and this connection performs some form of recognisable function. A system orders its world and simplifies the chaos that surrounds it. If you look around you will see systems everywhere as a way of naming things. Security; banking; air-conditioning; clothing; even razors have all been called systems (and it's become something of a hobby of mine to spot just how that word appears everywhere from the side of buses to toothpaste tubes). Systems are inescapable; ubiquitous.

Second whilst systems are an integral part of life in the *Age of Dispersion* (from the 1950s onwards), their use has a history that extends back behind the introduction of Cybernetics and Systems Theory alongside communication and computing systems in the 20th century through the 19th century and the mechanical systems like steam and photography of the industrial revolution to the 18th century. Three things happen at this time. First, system is given a definition in the first edition of Samuel Johnson's *Dictionary of the English Language*. Second, 'system' is established as a genre of writing[11] and as a way of understanding the production and organisation of knowledge, such as in Kant's appeal to systematicity in his three Critiques and the subsequent system(s) of German Idealism.[12] Third system became a means of social organisation underwriting modern forms of polity including liberal democracy, economics, law and education. Before this, in the 17th century, system is woven into the birth of modern science. The concluding book and overview to Newton's *Philosophiæ Naturalis, Principia Mathematica* is called, 'The System of the World.' In other words, the history of systems is an alternative way of narrating the history of modernity.

Be they infrastructural or metaphorical, systems are understood through the combinations of their component parts, operations and behaviour. Their whole is greater than the sum of their parts, as the cliché runs. Systems thinking is a way of thinking about the world in terms of emergent properties: that is wholes, rather than their constituent parts. It considers outputs and behaviours in terms of function, communication and control.

We know that you don't understand an ant colony by looking at a single ant any more than staring at a Euro coin helps you understand the economy. Knowing how the gears on a bike work doesn't explain the Tour de France, and human consciousness is not reducible to mere synapses snapping in the soft-machine of the brain. Each of these is complex entities that are better described when considered as systems that display distributed behaviour. The behaviour of the ant colony is dispersed throughout its system.[13] Our memories are not located in individual parts of our brains but rather spread across neural and even social networks.

Artists are obliged to work with systems. Some know this; some choose this situation; others pretend to be oblivious. But like it or not, every time something is exhibited, published, photographed, printed, written about, insured, sold, tweeted or whatever else happens to art these days, it is circulated within systems of dispersion, distribution and display. Artists use systems because of what they do. After all, mediums like sculpture and painting are complex structures with their own particular patterns of self-organisation. But there are other systems that artists can also use as mediums: technology; architecture; bodies; language; styles; and objects. These are systems too. Sometimes these systems are in plain view; at other times they are hidden. In the examples in this book, some of these systems are pulled from their often occulted obscurity, given aesthetic form and offered up for interrogation. Despite superficial differences between the works, they all share an underlying preoccupation with systems as a way of thinking about structure, relation, context, communication and technology.

The Age of Dispersion

This current era of systems and dispersion has been given different names. For Frederic Jameson, it was the 'age of the world system' (1992); Manuel Castells *The Network Society* (2000); and *The Postmodern Condition* by many others including JF Lyotard (1984). In each account, the economic, social and technological circumstances of late capitalism are coupled with the forms of knowledge and subjectivity that are produced by these conditions.

All of these definitions relate to social conditions developing in the second half of the 20th century coupled with the cultural and historical influence of electronic technologies such as computing and telecommunication systems. This leads to both the subsequent dominance of information as a metaphor for communication and organisation and in particular new configurations of those social systems that were established in modernity including: the economy; law; education; and forms of modern liberal democracy.

After the Second World War, new processes of production began to emerge out of the joint influences of the peacetime application of military research and development (including radar and telecommunication) and the necessity to rebuild societies. These post-industrial and post-Fordist processes are essentially inseparable from a global system of the transfer of materials, goods, services and data.[14]

For instance, the phenomena of containerisation followed the invention of the modern container in 1956 and its adoption in the subsequent decade. It is based on a standard sized entity or unit that could be easily transferred between ships, trains and trucks. Before then, it didn't make sense to manufacture things in other places to avail of cheaper resources and labour. Containers rendered everything transferable in a global system: raw materials; products; even people subject to trafficking. The container ship made capital truly migratory on a global scale and radically changed the nature of trade in a global network that transcended nation states. Dramatic changes in labour and employment were brought about by new technologies including mechanised production and computing. In the early 1970s, the Americans abandoned the gold standard which, along with the collapse of the Bretton Woods System of international economic management, heralded the subsequent market fundamentalism of neo-liberalism and its logic of deregulation and privatisation in a system of economic trading underwritten by the logic of speculation. It is no coincidence that this occurred alongside the military-industrial-cultural complex's development of telecommunication and computing networks including the internet (and its predecessor Arpanet) and the World Wide Web (in the early 1990s), which facilitated the rapid and massive exchange of information across global systems of communication and surveillance.

These technological developments coincided with the power of nation states becoming effaced by global systems of communication and control where capital migrated into information which, subsequently, became the primary unit of capitalist exchange. In such cultures, power no longer operates according to a disciplinary logic of modernity (as Foucault argued), but rather control where power is distributed across networks and 'ultra-rapid forms of free-floating control [have] replaced the old disciplines operating in the time frame of a closed system'[15] as Deleuze claimed in his famous essay 'Postscript on the Societies of Control.'

These effects of production and power create new experiences of subjectivity which, like information, is similarly understood to be both distributed and dispersed across different communicative networks and also produced and mediated by them. Hence, in the *Age of Dispersion,* human identity does not exist a priori to the processes of its production but rather emerges from the ecology of social, historical and material conditions, such as economic transactions, communication systems and social media, within which it is positioned. In other words, subjectivity does not pre-exist processes of power and production, but is instead constituted by them. It is *dispersed.*

The conditions of the *Age of Dispersion* present radical challenges to the accounts of, on the one hand, the autonomous and rational humanity that emerges in the European Enlightenment, and on the other art; or rather those aesthetic products and experiences that humanity produces and experiences its subjectivity through. As in other, and related, accounts of the conditions of subjectivity in late capitalism, such as Posthumanism and The Anthropocene, humans are identified as enmeshed within and reliant upon existing economic, technological and ecological networks that are beyond their control. The *Age of the Dispersion* thus suggests a political necessity for forms of cultural production to mimic its effects, map its operations and reveal its conditions in order to open it up for critique and the proposal of alternatives.

Technology, Identity and Self-Understanding

A common understanding of the word technology is as a technique, methodology or knowledge. It has been common throughout history for humans to understand who and what they are in relation to prevailing technology. In early Greek and Christian societies where the dominant technology related predominately to agriculture, humans were clay infused with spirit. In the 3rd century BCE, humans related themselves to hydraulic engineering; now, the human was understood as the site of canals and pipes for liquids such as the four humours. In the 16th century, humans became machines; that is, automata of cogs, gears and springs, whilst in the following centuries, metaphors of chemistry, steam power and then electricity were used.

The model of the human as a computer subsequently emerged as the dominant metaphor for cognition and behaviour with the establishment of the so-called von Neumann architecture, which provides the conceptual model of more or less all existing computers. This understands the human through a dualism in which the body is a piece of organic hardware that processes information about the world. From this perspective, thought is a type of software that decodes or represents the world through its own processes of simulation.

Each of these technologies and metaphors for humanity comes with their own potentials and restrictions. They each place humans within a particular worldview with a particular horizon. Each world will have its own limit.

Systems and dispersion are also related to particular technological conditions and precipitate another paradigm shift. They follow the logic of The Cloud and The Stack. They are a way of taking the world, thinking about it, manipulating it and doing things in it. Within systems, human subjects are conceived of as the outcome of dispersed relations within those systems.

Thinking in systems and dispersion means considering phenomena in terms of information and relations rather than objects. When both art and the human subject are understood through systems, the idea that either is the expression of either a set of universal human values or an autonomous instance of individual expression needs to be jettisoned. Instead, they are both objects and subjects that are radically distributed and dispersed across systems of communication and control. The pioneer of Second-Order Cybernetics, Gregory Bateson, described its subject matter as not objects or events but the: 'information 'carried' by events and objects. We consider the objects or events only as proposing facts, propositions, messages, percepts and the like.'[16]

Systems give us another technique alongside art, for thinking about who we are. This requires understanding that our individuality is positioned within a complex set of technological and environmental coordinates. Humanity is positioned within broader systems such as history, culture, language, architecture, economics, chemistry and physics. The human body is just one, biological, system amongst many others. Some of these are necessary for our existence; others are oblivious.

In an interview with *Women's Own* magazine in 1987, Margaret Thatcher made one of her most contentious and notorious claims:

And, you know, there's no such thing as society. There are individual men and women and there are families. And no government can do anything except through people, and people must look after themselves first.[17]

Thatcher could not have been more wrong. All people *are* is their relations. All of us get our identities from the systems we are dispersed throughout. And this is no cause for alarm, but rather a thrilling opportunity to rethink who, what and why we are at this moment.

Notes

1 Seth Price, 'Dispersion', in Beatrix Ruf & Axel Hochdörfer (eds.) *Social Synthetic* (Cologne: Koenig Books, 2017) pp. 67–85; pg. 68.

2 Seth Price, 'Dispersion,' in Beatrix Ruf & Axel Hochdörfer (eds.) *Social Synthetic* (Cologne: Koenig Books, 2017) pp. 67–85; pg. 71.

3 Described in the *Art Review Power 100* as being the 29th most influential entity in the art world in 2021 and 'a brand name through commercial partnerships and celebrity supporters that few can match' at: https://artreview.com/artist/kaws/?year=2021.

4 Kenneth Ewart Boulding, *The World as a Total System* (Beverly Hills, CA: Sage, 1985), pg. 9.

5 Stafford Beer, cited by Hugh Dubberly in, 'A Systems Literacy Manifesto' (Oct 2015) at: http://www.dubberly.com/articles/a-systems-literacy-manifesto.html (accessed, 10th March 2021).

6 https://www.ikea.com/ie/en/cat/storage-solution-systems-46052/ (accessed, 10th March 2021).

7 In 2015 data processing used 416.2 terawatt hours (TWh) of electricity or about 3 percent of the world's electricity and 2 percent of total global emissions. Google used 5.7 TWh. This represents more electricity the whole United Kingdom (300 (TWh)) and the same carbon footprint as the aviation industry. See James Bridle, *New Dark Age* (London: Verso, 2019). Similarly, the energy demands of virtual block-chain currencies such as Bitcoin are immense and will only increase as the production of the currency slows down. The Economist recently reported that that the power use for the servers that produce the software for Bitcoin software is at least 22 TWh per year which is about the same as Ireland. The Economist Group Limited, 'Why Bitcoin Uses so Much Energy,' *The Economist* (Jul. 9th, 2018) at: https://www.economist.com/ (accessed, 2nd June 2022).

8 'The Cloud Begins with Coal – Big Data, Big Networks, Big Infrastructure, and Big Power,' (2013) at: https://www.tech-pundit.com (accessed, 10th March 2021).

9 James Ball, *The System: Who Owns the Internet, and How It Owns Us* (London: Bloomsbury, 2020) pg. 3.

10 These figures come from Hemanshu Nigam, who runs online safety consultancy SSP Blue and was former chief security officer of MySpace, quoted in Adrian Chen, 'The Laborers Who Keep Dick Pics and Beheadings Out of Your Facebook Feed' at: https://www.wired.com (accessed, 2nd June 2022).

11 Clifford Siskin, *System* (Cambridge: MIT Press, 2017).

12 'By as early as 1837–1838, only a few years after Hegel's death, and still during Schelling's lifetime, Carl Ludwig Michelet published the two-volume *Geschichte der letzten Systeme der Philosophie in Deutschland von Kant bis Hegel (History of the Latest Systems of Philosophy in Germany from Kant to Hegel)*, thereby grouping these four philosophers and their works within a determinate epoch of German philosophy' Brian O'Connor and Georg Mohr (eds.), *German Idealism: An Anthology and Guide* (Chicago, IL: University of Chicago Press, 2007).

13 Bert Hölldobler and Edward O. Wilson, *The Superorganism* (New York: W. W. Norton & Company, 2009).

14 These ubiquitous systems of everyday life are undergirded by the prevailing myth of data as proposed by Claude Shannon in his theory of Information. Information

Theory was formulated by Shannon with Warren Weaver in the aftermath of the 2nd World War, as what they called a mathematical theory of communication. Claude Shannon, 'A Mathematical Theory of Communication,' *Bell System Technical Journal*, 27 (July & October, 1948) pp. 379–423 & 623–656.

15 Giles Deleuze, 'Postscript on the Societies of Control,' *October*, 59 (Winter, 1992) pp. 3–7 (5 pages).

16 Gregory Bateson, 'Cybernetic Explanation' reprinted in *Steps to an Ecology of Mind*, New Edition (Chicago, IL: Chicago University Press, 2000) pg. 410.

17 'Margaret Thatcher a Life in Quotes,' *The Guardian* (Mon. 8th April, 2013) at: https://www.theguardian.com/politics/2013/apr/08/margaret-thatcher-quotes (accessed, June 2022).

References

Ball, James, *The System: Who Owns the Internet, and How It Owns Us*, London: Bloomsbury, 2020

Bateson, Gregory, *Steps to an Ecology of Mind*, Chicago, IL: University of Chicago Press, 1972

Boulding, Kenneth Ewart, *The World as a Total System*, Beverly Hills, CA: Sage, 1985

Bridle, James, *New Dark Age*, London: Verso, 2019

Chen, Adrian, 'The Laborers Who Keep Dick Pics and Beheadings Out of Your Facebook Feed' (October 23, 2014) https://www.wired.com (accessed, 2nd June 2022)

Deleuze, Giles, 'Postscript on the Societies of Control', *October*, 59 (Winter, 1992, The MIT Press), pp. 3–7

Dubberly, Hugh, 'A Systems Literacy Manifesto' (Oct. 2015) http://www.dubberly.com/articles/a-systems-literacy-manifesto.html

Hölldobler, Bert and Edward O. Wilson, *The Superorganism*, New York: W. W. Norton & Company, 2009

O'Connor, Brian and Georg Mohr (ed.), *German Idealism: An Anthology and Guide*, Chicago, IL: University of Chicago Press, 2007

Price, Seth, 'Dispersion', in Beatrix Ruf & Axel Hochdörfer (eds.) *Social Synthetic*, Cologne: Koenig Books, 2017, pp. 67–85

Shannon, Claude, 'A Mathematical Theory of Communication', *Bell System Technical Journal*, 27 (July & October, 1948) pp. 379–423 & 623–656

Siskin, Clifford, *System*, Cambridge: MIT Press, 2017

1   The Aesthetics of Dispersion

Anything could be art, today. The modernist faith in medium specificity has been replaced by a widespread artistic and critical reticence to commit to particular mediums. What this means is that the materials as well as the methods available to the contemporary practitioner are so diverse that any historical specificity of the formal conditions of established mediums such as painting, sculpture, and performance is no longer guaranteed. This condition of medium agnosticism means that art is now, as Hal Foster puts it, the 'paradigm of no paradigm.'[1] For Arthur Danto, this has been the case since the historical turning point of art in the 1960s, when Minimalism first emerged, and after which 'there is no special way works of art have to be.'[2] At the National College of Art and Design, Dublin where I work, there is still a department of Painting, in the anachronistically named School of Fine Art, but the work that a student studying there might produce could just as easily be a performance as it might be an installation, digital work, text, sound-work or something else entirely (Figure 1.1).

Since its inception in 1955, *dOCUMENTA* has given some insight into the conditions of contemporary art at a particular historical moment. This large-scale international exhibition of contemporary art has been held in Kassel, Germany, every five years since 1955. It was originally set up in the aftermath of the Second World War in Western Germany but very close to the border with the Eastern Bloc as an expression of the spirit of contemporary art and Western cultural confidence although subsequent iterations have taken on a more self-critical awareness of the global contexts for contemporary art.

In *dOCUMENTA (13)* (2012), directed by Carolyn Christov-Bakargiev, three pieces, in particular, exemplified the dispersed and eclectic conditions of contemporary art introduced here. These pieces comprised: a breeze; a statement of withdrawal; and a somewhat grotty parkland. In each case, the specific medium or even focus of aesthetic attention was unclear, and attention was diverted towards the various environmental and institutional systems of support that the art was dispersed throughout.

Ryan Gander's work *I need some meaning I can Memorise (The Invisible Pull)* (2012) was exhibited in the ground floor of the central space, the

DOI: 10.4324/9781003315322-2

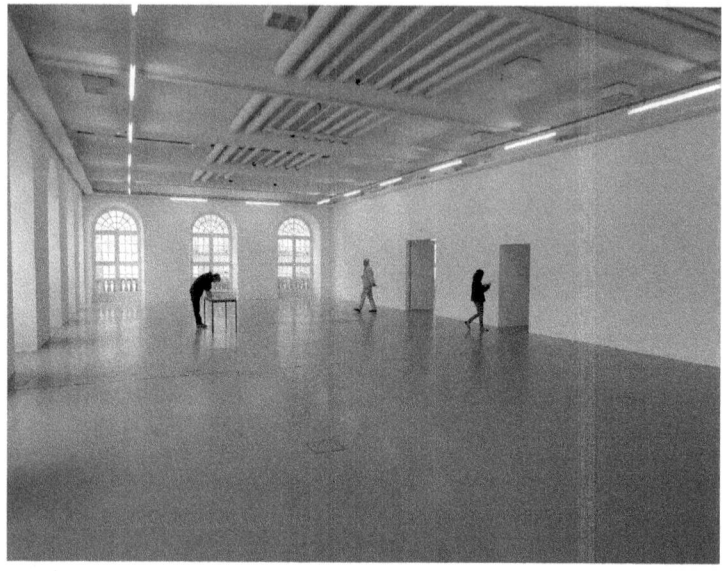

Figure 1.1 Museum Fridericianum at dOCUMENTA (13)

Kunsthalle Fridericianum. Being merely a soft breeze that wafted through the space, it was barely perceptible; not so strong as to be immediately obvious or evidently artificially created, yet not weak enough to be ignored. Within this same space was a horizontal vitrine containing several pages of a handwritten letter and the title label reading: 'A letter to Carolyn Christov-Bakargiev by Kai Althoff, May 24, 2011. Exhibited on the initiative of Carolyn Christov-Bakargiev and with the permission of the artist' with the title in German also included. This gesture was a statement of aesthetic withdrawal in which the painter, Kai Althoff, explains how, after a process of deliberation that they were not able to participate in the exhibition giving, amongst the reasons, the explanation that '"life" was more important.' Outside of this central exhibition space and some distance away was Pierre Huyghe's *Untilled* (2011–2012) installed in the Karlsaue Park. Huyghe claimed that the medium for his work was 'live things and inanimate things, made and not made.' It included a compost heap as home for insects such as ladybirds, the odd tortoise and the replanting of many plants, including marijuana and poisonous fruits providing an environment for: a figurative stone sculpture of a nude woman with a live beehive for a head; an emaciated, white Podenco Canario dog with a pink leg that seemed to live at the site; and all the curious human visitors to the installation (Figure 1.2).

The central presentation for the whole exhibition, in the Kunsthalle Fridericianum, included material that was not made to be seen as art including

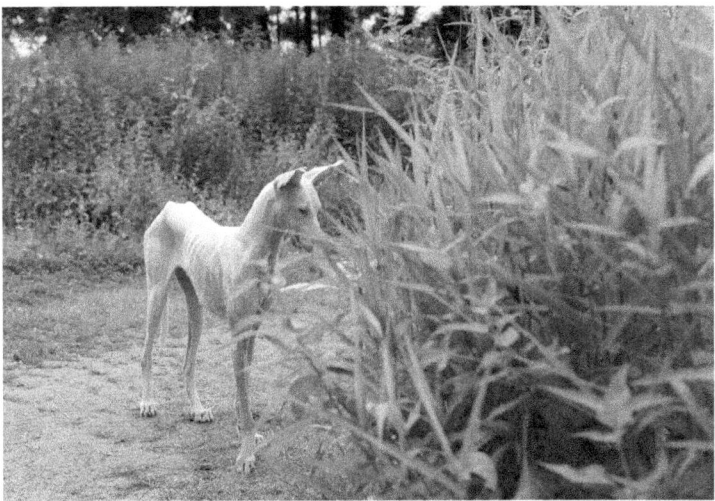

Figure 1.2 Untilled, Pierre Huyghe at dOCUMENTA (13)

three of the vases Morandi painted images of from 1949 onwards; a selection of artefacts taken by Lee Miller from Hitler's apartment (a perfume bottle, make-up compact and monogrammed towel); and objects from the National Museum in Beirut originally made of metal, glass ivory and terracotta that had been fused together during the war from 1975 to 1990 when the museum was on the frontline of hostilities.

Christov-Bakargiev explained how the whole exhibition was to challenge the 'boundary' between what is art and what is not:

> driven by a holistic and non-logocentric vision that is shared with, and recognises, the knowledges of animate and inanimate makers of the world. The attempt is to not put human thought hierarchically above the ability of other species and things to think or produce knowledge… What these participants do, and what they exhibit, in dOCUMENTA (13), may or may not be art. However, their acts, gestures, thoughts and knowledges produce and are produced by circumstances that are readable by art, aspects that art can cope with and absorb.[3]

In her curatorial statement, Christov-Bakargiev demonstrated total disinterest in respecting the boundaries between art and other things. This disinterest highlights a key feature of contemporary practices, namely that anything can be exhibited in the spaces of art and there is no material or aesthetic distinction between what is art and what is not. Her selections show that in contemporary practices, three elements of art that were historically certain are called into question: discrete works of art as the focus of specific aesthetic attention; artistic mediums with specific constitutive elements and protocols for their use; and the role of artists as engaging in a particular type of activity (making art) in a particular type of place (studios and galleries).

Dispersed Objects

The contemporary conditions of art in play at dOCUMENTA (13) are exemplified in the ongoing *e-flux* project created by Anton Vidokle in 2008. It is a platform for publishing, news, advertising, curating and other activities relating to contemporary art. The project began as a means of using a relatively new means of communication, email, to distribute and disperse information about forthcoming art events. It grew from this into a system of information exchange involving over 90,000 subscribers who receive the information about activities in the art world (exhibitions, events, launches and so on), which is subsequently archived and made available for reference. Receiving the information is free, and the agencies, such as art institutions, wanting to make an announcement pay a fee. This network has now grown to include a variety of different stakeholders including public institutions, as well as commercial galleries (through Art-Agenda) and educational institutions (through Art & Education, which is run in collaboration with Artforum International). e-Flux now publishes the influential e-flux journal (online) alongside activities of public promulgation involving art, architecture, education and cognate practices.

Vidokle insists that from the beginning in 1999 as an email service *e-flux* is always an art practice. Such an art practice relies absolutely on the systems of distribution throughout which it is dispersed. Likewise Vidokle, as an artist, becomes a subject who is similarly dispersed through the same systems. Later in the same interview in response to the question as to whether *e-flux* is a work of art or a company he responded with:

> e-flux is a work of art that uses circulation both as form and content. I would not claim sole authorship. I suppose I started it, but I do not see myself as the author in a traditional sense – it has always been a collaboration[…] it's not some object you can display in a museum alongside a wall label with my name and date.[4]

Liam Gillick acknowledges this condition of uncertainty as underwriting the conditions under which he works. The term 'Contemporary Art' he claims, 'Does Not Account for That Which is Taking Place' precisely because the term is so flexible and emptied of specific meaning:

> The term *contemporary art* has historically implied a specific accommodation with a loose set of open-minded economic and political values

that are mutable, global, and general and therefore have sufficed as an all-encompassing description of what is being made now – wherever. But the flexibility of contemporary art is no longer sufficiently capable of encompassing all dynamic current art, if only because an increasing number of artists seek a radical differentiation.[5]

Here, Gillick is revisiting familiar arguments previously made about the end of art albeit in his oblique way that can often be hard to follow. For example, reflecting on the relationship between contemporary conditions of production and exchange in the era of post-war globalisation the art historian Hans Belting wrote about the limitations of a presupposed notion of art to best describe contemporary creative practices:

> The commonplace concept of art can no longer cope with this. Everyone knows that art with an implied capital A has meanwhile fragmented into a spectrum of resistant phenomena that are accepted as art long before we are able to define them.[6]

Belting was repeating his earlier observation that after modernism was an End to the History of Art,[7] a claim which was itself echoed in the similar claims of other commentators, such as Kuspit and Danto amongst many others.[8] The general position these arguments share is that the art historical moment of high modernism was an end point to a historical teleology of art. What followed in the wake of this terminus was the erosion of distinctions between specific mediums, a spirit of artistic pluralism and an irreversible collapse of any aesthetic and formal distinctions between what is art and what is not.

Thierry de Duve has also argued that this dispersion of the singularity of art was necessitated by the figure of the Readymade. Duchamp's gesture necessitated a shift in philosophical aesthetics from judgements on stylistic value to ones of ontology in which the question of 'is this beautiful?' is replaced by 'is this art?' and that the new polymorphous forms of art in the wake of the avant-garde in which the boundaries between art and non-art dissolved should be considered, 'art in general.'[9]

Given his debt to Kant, de Duve's claim for the indeterminacy of art is experienced and expressed in terms of a sensual, that is aesthetic, judgement. Peter Osborne makes a similar designation but in temporal terms in his use of the term *Post-Contemporary*. By this, Osborne means that contemporary practices have become separated from any particular historical period or associated style. Art is instead understood through a set of situational rather than stylistic conditions, which are: 'the historical-ontological condition for the production of contemporary art in general - art, that is, that can sustain the signifiers "art" and "contemporary" in the deepest theoretical senses.'[10] In contrast to other art historical categories like Renaissance and Baroque, which have identifiable stylistic, historical and geographical characteristics,

Post-Contemporary Art is 'a radically distributive – that is, irreducibly relational – unity of the individual artwork across the totality of its multiple material instantiations, at any particular time.'[11]

Artistic Systems

As both de Duve and Seth Price observe, Duchamp's *Readymades*, and in particular, their subsequent rediscovery and adoption from the 1950s onwards, rendered it impossible for artists to act obliviously to the relationships between art and the institutional frames of the systems of art history, criticism, museums and markets. This has now left art in its contemporary circumstance of ontological and aesthetic instability. Or, simply, anything can now be art and, as a result, the status of something being accepted as art is entirely dependent upon it being positioned, observed and dispersed within systems of relations.

This preoccupation with systems has a long tail, and there are other uses of systems by artists. Consider, for example, the use of the grid in many early modernist practices such as Piet Mondrian, Paul Klee, Hilma af Klint and later artists such as Ad Reinhardt, Sol LeWitt and Carl Andre.[12] This can also be interpreted as modern predilection towards systems where structure and form are presented and interrogated as primary subject matter in place of expressive, mimetic, symbolic or representational content.

Or consider painting as a medium that has long pre-existed computer technologies, but which is still, inherently, systemic. Writing on contemporary painting, David Joselit claims that 'the most important problem to be addressed on canvas since Warhol'[13] is 'How does painting belong to a network?'[14] The painter Martin Kippenberger's statement addresses the same problem:

> 'Simply to hang a painting on the wall and say that it's art is dreadful. The whole network is important! ... When you say art, then everything possible belongs to it. In a gallery that is also the floor, the architecture, the color of the walls.'[15]

Kippenberger's injunction involves questioning how painting might take on the challenge of photography (along with other technologies for image making), whilst making that challenge explicitly part of its artistic content. Consider, for example, how works by Wade Guyton and Sarah Morris challenge the logics of image making and distribution across systems. As Joselit observes: 'Certainly, painting has always belonged to networks of distribution and exhibition, but Kippenberger claims something more: that, by the early 1990s, an individual painting should explicitly visualize such networks.'[16]

However, even though Joselit is talking about painting in the 1990s, its reliance upon a system of relations is considerably older than that. The emergence of art as a system was part of the logic and aesthetic of modernism from at least as early as the middle of the 19th century. It is evident Édouard Manet's adoption of motifs from Raphael, Titian and Giorgione in *Le Déjeuner sur l'herbe* (1863) and *Olympia* (1863); and Pablo Picasso's later echoing of El Greco in *Les Demoiselles d'Avignon* (1907) or his obsessive series of 58 interpretations of Velázquez's *Las Meninas* (1957).

Such appropriative gestures self-consciously perform the artists' awareness that a medium such as painting is also a system of accumulated techniques, materials and references. Such systems have become historically sedimented into all the mediums of art. These systems are both the horizon of expectations that form the environment that artists work within and the 'technical support' (as Rosalind Krauss characterises mediums) they have to hand to make art.

Dispersed Relations

Thus far I have proposed that art in the *Age of Dispersion* take relations in systems as both their medium and primary subject matter; and that this dispersion of art and artists into systems of relations leads to both stylistic and ontological uncertainty. The *Aesthetics of Dispersion* might, thus, also provide an alternative re-description of a dominant paradigm in contemporary art practices from the last 25 years which the curator Nicolas Bourriaud named *Relational Aesthetics*.

Relational Aesthetics is now most often associated with a particular style of collaborative and participatory practices. It emerged from the collective practice of a group of artists who came to prominence in Europe in the 1990s. Bourriaud identified that such practices operate within 'the realm of human interactions and its social context rather than the assertion of an independent and private symbolic space.'[17] In doing so, he argues, they place an: 'emphasis on a parallel engineering, on open forms based on the affirmation of the trans-individual.'[18]

For Bourriaud, the potential of such practices lies in how they can represent contemporary conditions of subjectivity. Hence Bourriaud proposes that through participating in relations, art can participate in social systems. Relational practices are inherently and necessarily systemic and dispersed and include such paradigmatic gestures as Rirkrit Tiravanija's *Untitled (Free)*, in which he created a kitchen in 303 Gallery in New York and gave away Thai curry and rice and hosted events; or the collaboration between Douglas Gordon and Philippe Parreno with the Scottish band Mogwai on *Zidane: A 21st Century Portrait* (2006), a documentary focusing solely on the soccer player during a single match.

George Baker's critique of Relational Aesthetics is that it produces art indistinguishable from leisure and entertainment and is, therefore, 'a compensatory move in the face of the overwhelming lack of relationality in contemporary social life.'[19] In this interpretation, art becomes indistinguishable from and dispersed into other spaces of entertainment, commerce and spectacle.

This is exemplified by James Turrell, *Akhob*, in the Louis Vuitton store in Las Vegas where audiences get a completely immersive experience as they are absorbed by what Turrell calls, his Ganzfeld or complete light field. The Louis Vuitton store is located in a shopping mall where forms of entertainment and forms of commerce become indistinguishable from one another.

This is all underwritten by what Foucault famously observed lies at the heart of neo-liberalism and the burgeoning gig economy which is the coupling of creativity with entrepreneurship and 'the replacement every time of homo oeconomicus as a partner of exchange with homo oeconomicus as an entrepreneur of himself, being for himself his own capital, being for himself his own producer, being for himself the source of his own earnings.' Such a figure is exemplified in the figure of the migrant who, Foucault observes, embodies, literally, the migration of human capital across the global system: 'Migration is an investment; the migrant is an investor. He is an entrepreneur of himself who incurs expenses by investing to obtain some kind of improvement.'[20] These conditions are epitomised by the contemporary artist who lives and works in multiple locations whilst also exhibiting their work in fairs and galleries around the world.

A related critique is that relational practice merely replicates forms of neo-liberal sociality. For example in a discussion on Rirkrit Tiravanija, Claire Bishop contended that his own projects of cooking Thai curries in gallery spaces and inviting people in to participate in those events were no more than 'self-congratulatory entertainment.' Tiravanija countered that Bishop's attitude in itself reflects a kind of 'academic racism' that thwarts European and North American facing criticism and art history from understanding the significance of sharing food in Thai Buddhist culture and that the project is evoking different histories and different forms of conviviality.

The *Aesthetics of Dispersion* potentially doesn't merely passively participate in the spectacle and entertainment of late capitalism. Instead, through taking on and mimicking some of the effects of dispersion of late capitalism it also offers a critique of them by revealing the contingency of those conditions. It also, through the creation of communities of experience, offers something of a bulwark against them.

Systems of Distribution

The problem with art that is absolutely indeterminate or post contemporary is that it is potentially too slippery to allow for a firm art historical grasp on it. In the absence of medium, style or period, it becomes a challenge to identify what, precisely, one is describing or archiving. As I have argued elsewhere,[21] the concept of system when understood as a medium for art provides some art historical consistency to the radically distributive character of art practices after modernism. Considered in terms of systems, art is now understood as something which is *dispersed* throughout systems and not specific objects granted specific types of attention. Writing in 1969, Jack Burnham identified the artistic move from object to system as being coupled with technological developments, in particular computing and telecommunications. He wrote:

> A major illusion of the art system is that art resides in specific objects. Such artefacts are the material basis for the concept of the 'work of art.' But in essence, all institutions which process art data, thus making information, are components of the work of art. Without the support system, the object ceases to have definition; but without the object, the support system can still sustains the notion of art. So we can see why the art experience attaches itself less and less to canonical or given forms but embraces every conceivable experiential mode, including living in everyday environments.[22]

David Joselit and Lane Relyea have also examined the relationships between technologies and mediums through the vocabularies of systems and networks. Joselit claims that the new screen technologies of pads and phones create a freedom of images, which leads to a situation where contemporary art is determined by format rather than medium. Format, Joselit argues, is 'a heterogeneous and often provisional structure that channels content.' Formats are opposed to objects that are characterised by 'discernible limits and relative stability [which] lend themselves to singular meanings' and they 'regulate image currencies (image power) by modulating their force, speed, and clarity.' 'After art,' Joselit explains, 'comes the logic of networks where links can cross space, time, genre and scale in surprising and multiple ways.'[23]

With a similar focus on systems of distribution, for Relyea contemporary art is characterised by: 'the rise to dominance of network structures and behaviours and their enabling manifestations: the database, the platform, the project and the free agent or do-it-youselfer.'[24] A consequence of what Relyea identifies is the blurring of the lines between artist, cultural agent and entrepreneur with the effect that the identifiable figure of the artist along with their productions becomes *dispersed* and distributed into the systems of contemporary life.

Dispersed Subjects

I am proposing, then, that considering contemporary art through the logic of systems and dispersion offers some consistency and coherence to a set of practices that are otherwise stylistically and conceptually diffuse. However, the vocabulary of systems calls into question two preconceptions about the identity of both art and humans. First, it requires a recalibration in thinking about what works of art are be they, on the one hand, representations of the appearance of the world; or, on the other, as instances of self-expression. Second, it also means we need to reconsider exactly what the humans that make and experience these artworks are too. This is because any understanding of what art is will always be underwritten by correlated view of what a human being is. This relationship between subjectivity and art hinges upon technology, as a set of techniques, as a mediator between the two. This equivalence is most clearly evident in art. For example, in the humanist model of art, exemplified in the Western European Renaissance, the artwork is understood as an expression of trans-historical values predicated on the universality of human reason. This was described by Erwin Panofsky in his account of the history of art as what he called a 'Humanistic Discipline' (1940) enacted through the method of Iconology (the meticulous decoding of the original meaning of symbols in art). Thus, Panofsky addressed the problem of how the contemporary historian can confront historical objects without merely projecting their own values back onto them. What, Panofsky asks, is the Archimedean point or immoveable value that counteracts such projection? His solution was an art historical method that was underwritten by a faith in shared human reason that bridges the gap between different historical times and places. Thus, Panofsky's art historical method of Iconology is illustrative of his own Humanism; a Humanism he saw as being paralleled in Renaissance values and worldview. On the one hand, this understands works of art as being meaningful historical documents that can be meaningfully interpreted precisely because they are the product of a process of human rationality. And on the other hand, this understands human subjects as also participating in a process of human rationality that is not culturally or historically specific, hence their ability to understand the meanings of objects that are not culturally or historically specific to their own milieu.

A very different model of both art and subjectivity is found in the Expressionist model of art that is often coupled with one tendency of Western modernism. This understands art not as the product of shared human values but as the index of a unique and individual expressive act. Wilhelm Worringer writing in *Abstraction and Empathy* (1997) about an elemental and fundamental human urge at artistic expression writes that the instinctive 'urge to abstraction' happens without the intervention of the intellect:

> because intellect had not yet dimmed instinct, the disposition to regularity, which after all is already present in the germ-cell, was able to find the appropriate abstract expression. These regular abstract forms are, therefore, the only ones and the highest, in which man can rest in the face of the vast confusion of the world-picture.[25]

This was not only one of the foundational texts for German Expressionism but also exemplary of one, dominant, trend within concurrently emergent artistic modernism predicated on self-expression and abstraction. In contrast to the humanist subject who participates in some collective project the modern subject is the individual, autonomous and expressive agent who is also offered the promise of an articulation of their identity in the systems of modernity including the systems of politics, law, education and the economy.[26]

To bring this to bear on a third example, the art and human subject that exemplifies the aesthetics of dispersion is neither the expression of a set of universal human values, nor an autonomous instance of individual expression. Instead, a different model of subjectivity is presented. Contemporary art is characterised by a lack of confidence in the autonomy of art as an especial focus of human attention; likewise, the identities of its corollary human subjects are equally diffuse. In the *Age of Dispersion*, both objects and subjects are distributed across systems of communication and control.

Notes

1 Hal Foster, *Design and Crime: And Other Diatribes* (London: Verso, 2010) pg. 128.

2 Arthur C. Danto, *After the End of Art: Contemporary Art and the Pale of History* (Princeton, NJ: Princeton Univ. Press, 1998) pg. 47.

3 Carolyn Christov-Bakargiev, *dOCUMENTA 13* (Ostfildern: Hatje cantz Verlag, 2012) pg. 31.

4 Interview: Anton Vidokle of e-flux originally published at: https://www.dossierjournal.com/read/interviews/interview-anton-vidokle-of-e-flux/ archived at: http://archive.is/rREiH#selection-335.0-335.34 (2009) (accessed, 14th May 2018).

5 Liam Gillick, *Industry and Intelligence: Contemporary Art since 1820* (New York: Columbia University Press, 2016) pg. 1.

6 Hans Belting, *Art History After Modernism* (trans. Saltzwedel et al.) (Chicago, IL: The University of Chicago Press, 2003) pg. 4.

7 Hans Belting, *The End of the History of Art* (trans. Wood) (Chicago, IL: University of Chicago Press, 1987).

8 Donald Kuspit, *The End of Art* (Cambridge: Cambridge University Press, 2005); Arthur Danto, *After the End of Art* (rev. ed.) (Princeton, NJ: Princeton University Press, 2014); Eva Guelen, *The End of Art: Readings in a Rumor after Hegel* (Stanford University Press, 2006); Suzi Gablik, *Has Modernism Failed*, (London: Thames and Hudson, 1984); Victor Burgin, *The End of Art Theory* (London: Palgrave MacMillan, 1986).

9 Thierry de Duve, *Kant after Duchamp* (Cambridge: MIT Press, 1997) pg. 73.

10 Peter Osborne, *Anywhere or Not At All: Philosophy of Contemporary Art* (London: Verso Books, 2013) pg. 51.

11 Peter Osborne, *Anywhere or Not At All: Philosophy of Contemporary Art* (London: Verso Books, 2013) pg. 48.

12 Rosalind Krauss, 'Grids' October, Vol. 9 (Summer, 1979, MIT Press), pp. 50–64 (15 pages).

13 David Joselit, "Painting Beside Itself", *October* 130 (Fall 2009, MIT Press) pp. 125–134; pg. 125.

14 Ibid., original emphasis.

15 One Has to Be Able to Take It!" Excerpts from an Interview with Martin Kippenberger by Jutta Koether, November 1990–May 1991,' in Ann Goldstein (ed.) *Martin Kippenberger: The Problem Perspective* (Los Angeles, CA: The Museum of Contemporary Art; Cambridge: MIT Press, 2008) pg. 316.

16 David Joselit, 'Painting Beside Itself', *October* 130 (Fall 2009, MIT Press) pp. 125–134; pg. 125.
17 Nicolas Bourriaud, *Relational Aesthetics* (Dijon: Les presses du réel, 1998) p. 113.
18 Nicolas Bourriaud, 'Berlin Letter about Relational Aesthetics', in Claire Docherty, *From Studio to Situation: From Studio to Situation* (London: Black Dog, 2004) (48–9) pp. 43–49.
19 George Baker, 'Relations and Counter-Relations, an Open Letter to Nicolas Bourriaud.'
20 Michel Foucault, *The Birth of Biopolitics* (ed. Michel Sennelart) (London: MacMillan, 2008) pg. 226/240.
21 *Systems of Art (Art, Art History and Systems-Theory)* (Oxford: Peter Lang, 2008); 'Actor-Network Aesthetics: The Conceptual Rhymes of Bruno Latour and Contemporary Art', in Muecke & Felski (eds.) *Latour and the Humanities* (Duke University Press) pp. 425–468; 'Art History as a System', in van Tuinen (ed.) *Speculative Art Histories* (Edinburgh: Edinburgh University Press, 2017) pp. 39–60.
22 Jack Burnham, 'Real Time Systems,' *Artforum* VIII, no. 1 (September 1969) pg. 50.
23 David Joselit, *After Art* (Princeton, NJ: Princeton University Press, 2012).
24 Lane Relyea, *Your Everyday Art World* (Cambridge: MIT Press, 2017).
25 Wilhelm Worringer, *Abstraction and Empathy* (trans. Michael Bullock) (Chicago, IL: Elephant, 1997) pg. 19.
26 These two different understandings of art and the human subject might not, necessarily, be mutually exclusive. The act of individual expression, for example, might be related to a general human impulse shared by all; just as the participation in a universal human rationality can be understood as a means of moving from the individual to the general, which is a mainstay of Kantian aesthetics. However, they do represent how different ways of understanding what a human is becomes manifest in different aesthetic practices that are specific to the historical and cultural contexts within which they are situated.

References

Baker, George, 'Relations and Counter-Relations, an Open Letter to Nicolas Bourriaud', in Yilmaz Dziewior (ed.) *Zusammenhänge herstellen/Contextualise* (pp. 126–133), Cologne: Dumont, 2002
Belting, Hans, *The End of the History of Art* (trans. Christopher Wood), Chicago, IL: University of Chicago Press, 1987
Belting, Hans, *Art History After Modernism* (trans. Caroline Saltzwedel et al.), Chicago, IL: The University of Chicago Press, 2003
Bourriaud, Nicolas, *Relational Aesthetics*, Dijon: Les presses du réel, 1998
Bourriaud, Nicolas, 'Berlin Letter about Relational Aesthetics', in Claire Docherty (ed.) *From Studio to Situation: From Studio to Situation*, London: Black Dog, 2004 pp. 43–49
Burgin, Victor, *The End of Art Theory*, London: Palgrave MacMillan, 1986
Burnham, Jack, 'Real Time Systems', *Artforum*, VIII, no. 1 (September 1969) pg. 50
Christov-Bakargiev, Carolyn, *dOCUMENTA 13*, Ostfildern: Hatje cantz Verlag, 2012
Danto, Arthur C., *After the End of Art: Contemporary Art and the Pale of History*, Princeton, NJ: Princeton University Press, 1998
de Duve, Thierry, *Kant after Duchamp*, Cambridge: MIT Press, 1997
Foster, Hal, *Design and Crime: and Other Diatribes*, London: Verso, 2010

Foucault, Michel, '14 March 1979' (pp. 215–237) and '21 March 1979' (pp. 239–265), in Michel Sennelart (ed.) *The Birth of Biopolitics*, London: MacMillan, 2008

Gablik, Suzi, *Has Modernism Failed*, London: Thames and Hudson, 1984

Gillick, Liam, *Industry and Intelligence: Contemporary Art Since 1820*, New York: Columbia University Press, 2016

Goldstein, Ann (ed.), *Martin Kippenberger: The Problem Perspective*, Los Angeles, CA: The Museum of Contemporary Art; Cambridge: MIT Press, 2008

Guelen, Eva, *The End of Art: Readings in a Rumor after Hegel*, Stanford: Stanford University Press, 2006

Halsall, Francis, *Systems of Art (Art, Art History and Systems-Theory)*, Oxford: Peter Lang, 2008

Halsall, Francis, 'Art History as a System', in Sjoerd van Tuinen (ed.), *Speculative Art Histories*, Edinburgh: Edinburgh University Press, 2017, pp. 39–60

Halsall, Francis, 'Actor-Network Aesthetics: The Conceptual Rhymes of Bruno Latour and Contemporary Art', in Stephen Muecke & Rita Felski (eds.) *Latour and the Humanities*, Duke University Press, 2021a, pp. 425–468

Joselit, David, 'Painting Beside Itself', *October*, Vol. 130, Fall 2009, MIT Press, pp. 125–134

Joselit, David, *After Art*, Princeton, NJ: Princeton University Press, 2012

Krauss, Rosalind, 'Grids', *October*, Vol. 9, Summer, 1979, MIT Press, pp. 50–64

Kuspit, Donald, *The End of Art*, Cambridge: Cambridge University Press, 2005

Osborne, Peter, *Anywhere or Not At All: Philosophy of Contemporary Art*, London: Verso Books, 2013

Relyea, Lane, *Your Everyday Art World*, Cambridge: MIT Press, 2017

Vidokle, Anton, 'Interview,' E-Flux, https://www.dossierjournal.com/read/interviews/interview-anton-vidokle-of-e-flux/ archived at: http://archive.is/rREiH#selection-335.0-335.34 (2009) (accessed, 14th May 2018)

Worringer, Wilhelm, *Abstraction and Empathy* (trans. Michael Bullock), Chicago, IL: Elephant, 1997

2   Seth Price and the Stuff of Systems

There is dominant strand within contemporary art that is underwritten by a particular understanding of what the human subject is. Both are characterised by dispersion throughout systems of communication and control. The term dispersion was borrowed from Seth Price's essay of the same name and which is one of his best known works. This work is considered along with some other examples concluding with *Folklore U.S.* (2011–2014) to argue that whilst, as Price acknowledges, his work sits within the horizon of Conceptual Art rather than being about the dematerialisation of art, it is ultimately concerned with exploring the physical supports of image production and the *re-materialisation* of art in the *Age of Dispersion*. In an inversion of the logic of conceptualism Price draws aesthetic attention to the materiality and *stuff* of things that are dispersed in systems.

Price identifies Conceptual Art as both the theoretical and historical horizon for his practice. But whilst conceptualism explored the dematerialisation of art through focusing on language, the reproducible image and the institutional supports for art, Price, however, explores those elements of materiality and distribution that are not explicitly associated with artistic mediums. Rather than the typical tendency of conceptualism to turn to language, photography and Institutional Critique leading to the dispersion of individual works of art into systems, Price focuses attention on the other side of the equation of Conceptual Art. His work foregrounds the physical correlates and media that otherwise might recede from aesthetic and critical attention. These are elements such as Mylar film, CNC-routed veneer, PDF files and videotapes that support and distribute images and texts. In arguing this, I claim that Price is following the cues of Robert Smithson who through his exploration of entropy, affect and materialisation offered an alternative trajectory for practice to those of modernist medium specificity and anti-art that stemmed from the dual influences of either Clement Greenberg or Marcel Duchamp.

From this first observation follow the two main claims of this chapter.

First, by exploring contemporary conditions of dispersed subjectivity Price not only offers a general portrait of human subjects in the *Age of Dispersion* but also provides something of a self-portrait in a mode that is neither

DOI: 10.4324/9781003315322-3

representational nor Expressionistic but rather mimetic of certain conditions of distributed identity and their material supports. That is, rather than attempting to represent subjects or subjectivity in the *Age of Dispersion*, Price mimics its effects on identity through his own strategies of dispersion. As he observes: 'New strategies are needed to keep up with commercial distribution, decentralization, and dispersion. You must fight something in order to understand it.'[1]

Second, I argue that through this drawing of attention to the material supports of distribution and dispersion one may use Price's work to consider the often occluded material conditions of the systems we inhabit.

Dispersed Subjectivity

Price has explicitly acknowledged dispersed subjectivity as a subject for his practice. In *Redistribution* (2007–present), Price made an audio-visual recording of a typical artist's talk. Typically, these talks introduce examples of work alongside influences, motivations and overarching themes all of which link the artist's practice to their identity as a unifying agency. However, in *Redistribution* any singular identity of the talker, or meaning of the talk, is undermined by the use of jarring graphics, background music, voice-overs and repetition, which sometimes make it hard to follow. Further, the piece remains in a process of adaptation as Price edits, adds and removes parts for different manifestations (public talks, video recordings, etc.). In this work, the form and content of the artwork become indistinguishable from one another; that is, the means by which the work is recorded and subsequently distributed is also its primary subject matter. And both are in flux.

The overall feeling of matters being in flux reappears in *Fuck Seth Price: A Novel* (New York: Leopard Press, 2015): an abstract novel written in a self-reflexive stream-of-consciousness style that Price once called 'slippery auto-fiction.' The subject seems to be an artist, much like Price, who spends the majority of the text considering both the condition of contemporary art and the construction and function of the novel itself. At the same time, he made *http://organic.software* (2015), which is an online database that he had originally produced anonymously. It contained a dataset of over 4,000 high-profile art collectors including images of faces, addresses, political donations, net worth and other information available online. In discussing both pieces, Price reflected on them as companion pieces and as portraits.

They're both written: one is a novel; the other is coded. One takes up a current literary form, the other looks like a social-media site. They were published in the same month. They're not art objects. They don't make money, they cost me money. The site was an exercise in making an anonymous and unpublicized artwork, while the title of the novel makes it the opposite of that. They both express a kind of negativity and aggression, obviously. They're publicly accessible, and they circulate outside the art world. At the same time, they both address a kind of local politics, in the sense of the art world as the world around me, the thing I know about, care about, can speak about and also implicate myself in, and all my feelings about that. But there's a level of fiction introduced; it's not a direct view. The novel is a slippery autofiction, and the website's About page has a fictional backstory for why there's this massive database of art collectors.[2]

In these examples, Price is presenting a portrait of the art world in 2015 along with a type of self-portrait.[3] However, these are portraits that are not representational in either iconic or expressive terms. They neither present any likeness of Price nor express any of his subjective states. Instead, by virtue of their distributed nature they are mimetic of the conditions of *dispersion* that characterise both works of art and human subjects in the *Age of Dispersion*.

Dispersion, the Essay

Price's most well-known work *Dispersion* (2002–ongoing)[4] began as an academic essay drawing on art historical and theoretical sources to reflect upon conditions of dispersion against the horizon of the emerging predominance of the internet. It was initially available in printed form but has since become widely available in digital form as a PDF and via online sources, as well as forming the basis for the installation *Essay with Knots* (2008) (Figure 2.1).

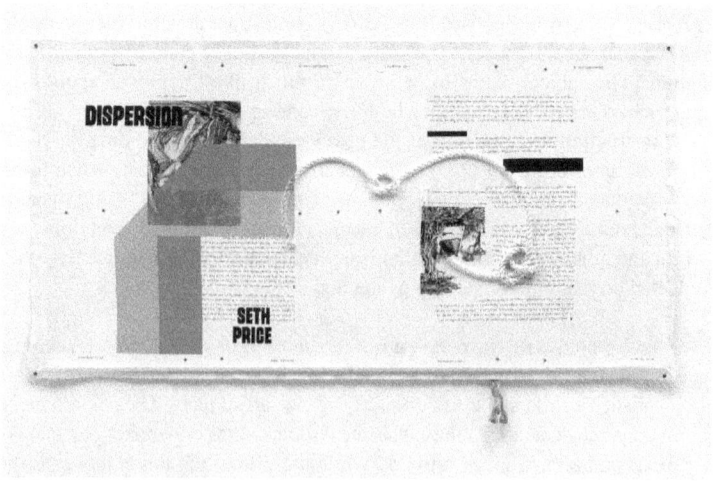

Figure 2.1 Seth Price: Essay with Knots: Alpha+Omega (2008)

In each iteration, *Dispersion* performs its dispersed nature as it declares its distribution over the numerous platforms by which it is presented. In the essay, Price poses the central question that forms the meaning of the work and which apply to both the object and the subject in play:

Suppose an artist were to release the work directly into a system that depends on reproduction and distribution for its sustenance, a model that encourages contamination, borrowing, stealing, and horizontal blur?[5]

Price claims his starting point is Conceptual Art which he identifies as a historical moment from the early 1970s that is still the dominant horizon for contemporary art. That is, Conceptual Art is a project that, for Price, remains both 'radically incomplete' and ubiquitous in that: 'today it seems that most of the work in the international art system positions itself as Conceptual to some degree, yielding the "Conceptual painter," the "DJ and Conceptual artist," the "Conceptual web artist."'[6]

As already discussed, *Dispersion* is ostensibly about the influence of Duchamp, and the figure of the Readymade, on art made over the last 50 years. In particular, this influence has rendered fluid and dispersed the once rigid borders that protected the separate and distinct identity and value of art. Now, when considered in relation to the fields of experience or use in which works of art may be positioned, such as communication, entertainment or economics, they are indistinguishable from other things in the world.

What Price takes from Duchamp is the artistic turn towards an interrogation of the systems of support, distribution and display that art takes place within. But he pivots away from the usual reading of Duchamp's significance to relating it specifically to new media and the Information Age:

Distributed media can be defined as social information circulating in theoretically unlimited quantities in the common market, stored or accessed via portable devices such as books and magazines, records and compact discs, videotapes and DVDs, personal computers and data diskettes. Duchamp's question has new life in this space, which has greatly expanded during the last few decades of global corporate *sprawl*. It's space into which the work of art must project itself lest it be outdistanced entirely by these corporate interests.[7]

Conceptual Art is frequently read according to the oppositional logic of the avant-garde. As such, through a turn to language (Linguistic Turn) and negation of aesthetics (Anti-Aesthetic) it operates as a form of Institutional Critique. In doing so, it is characterised as a critique of the hierarchical systems and power dynamics inherent in institutions and an attempt to undermine the individual art object as a privileged focus of aesthetic attention; a means of self-expression; or a valuable commodity. For this reason, Conceptual Art is often coupled with a critique of capitalism in general and the art market in particular such as in the work of Lawrence Weiner or the flourish of politically orientated use of conceptual gestures in South American art, especially from the late 1960s. Price, however, is interested in a different trajectory, that is with interrogating how art is reliant upon the distributive and dispersive systems of capitalism, such as music, design, fashion, graphic design and advertising in order to be experienced through portable formats such as, Price observes, '*books and magazines, records and compact discs, videotapes and DVDs*' and which now include screens, tablets and other devices. As Price puts it:

> It is useful to continually question the avant-garde's traditional romantic opposition to bourgeois society and values. The genius of the bourgeoisie manifests itself in the circuits of power and money that regulate the flow of culture. National bourgeois culture, of which art is one element, is based around commercial media, which, together with technology, design, and fashion, generate some of the important differences of our day. These are the arenas in which to conceive of a work positioned within the material and discursive technologies of distributed media.[8]

In other words, Price's work is not Neo-Avant-Garde or a continuation of practices that have proved either inert as forms of Institutional Critique, as seen in the work of Daniel Buren, or as bolstering rather than dismantling the form of the artwork as a commodity as can be seen in the co-option of the figure of the reproducible multiple without an original exemplified in the market-driven practices of Jeff Koons or Damien Hirst. Instead, Price's exploration of systems of dispersion continues the interrogation and redefinition of the relation between subjects and objects, which was always central to modernist self-reflexivity in general.

Whilst Duchamp is his stated starting point for Price's work in general and *Distribution* in particular, an equally important one is Robert Smithson who is alluded to both formally and theoretically. This influence goes largely unstated in *Distribution* aside from two brief mentions and an image of *Spiral Jetty* in some versions.[9] Elsewhere Price makes more specific use of Smithson. For example in *Digital Video Effect: 'Spills'* (2004), Price appropriates personal home video footage taken by Joan Jonas of Robert Smithson discussing the art market with Richard Serra and the art dealer Joseph Helman.[10]

In straightforwardly stylistic terms, *Dispersion* actually looks like a Smithson essay (Figure 2.2).

Formally, the presentation of *Distribution* recalls Smithson's published work from the late 1960s and early 1970s such as 'Spiral Jetty' and 'Quasi-Infinities and the Waning of Space.'[11] In the latter, Smithson accompanies blocks of text with black and white thumbnail images from a variety of historical sources such as Kepler's model of the universe and an installation shot of a Donald Judd wall piece. Likewise, *Distribution* includes black and white

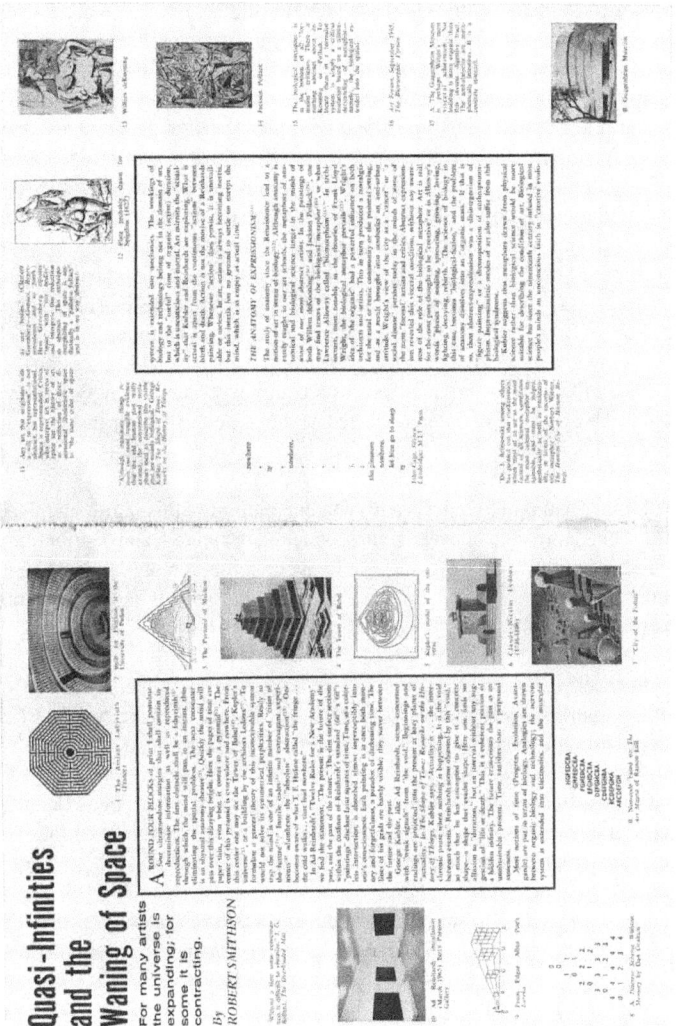

Figure 2.2 Robert Smithson: 'Quasi-Infinities and the Waning of Space,' *Arts Magazine* Vol. II (November 1966), first page

reproductions of a similar scale in relation to the text including Liam Gillick, *Legislation Discussion Platform* (1998); and Dürer, *Melancholia I* (1514).

However, I argue that it is Smithson's figure of the Site/Non-Site where his most significant influence on Price lies and it supersedes that of the Readymade in terms of conceptual significance. The Site/Non-Site establishes a dialectical relation between elements which, as I will also observe in relation to Gillick's work, are a process of constant deferral of attention away from any specific focus. In Smithson's work, the dialectic involved an abstract gallery installation that referred to a landscape along with the attendant geographical site such as *A Nonsite (Franklin, New Jersey)* (1968), which is a gallery installation of a sculpture with a receptacle containing limestone from the site along with a photographic print of the location. Smithson described the relationship between Site and Non-site as consisting of what he called a 'course of hazards' composed of a network of objects and signifiers including the site itself alongside: 'signs, photographs, and maps that belong to both sides of the dialectic at once. Both sides are present and absent at the same time.'[12]

In other words, instead of being a discrete object for aesthetic reflection the appearance of Site/Non-Site manifests as a complex, recursive and yet never fully graspable system of interconnected features across which meaning is dispersed. This is also how Price describes his own work:

> With more and more media readily available through this unruly archive, the task becomes one of packaging, producing, reframing, and distributing; a mode of production analogous not to the creation of material goods, but to the production of social contexts, using existing material. Anything on the internet is a fragment, provisional, pointing elsewhere.[13]

The influence of Smithson positions Price's work in a counter narrative to that of the dominant reception of Conceptual Art which is characterised by a linguistic turn; a dematerialisation of the art object; and a tendency towards an anti-aesthetic sensibility.

Price is explicit in foregrounding the materiality of his work. For example, his account of *Dispersion* prioritises the material over the textual, semiotic or conceptual elements of the work:

> People were starting to simply talk about Dispersion as an essay, which it's not. … It's the text, but it's also the package, the design, it's the circulation. That's why I wanted to print it on these big panels with the knots: then you have to look at it as art.[14]

This point is illustrated by *Essay with Knots* (2008) which is a sculptural installation in which the essay is re-presented across nine wall-mounted panels of vacuum-formed plastic incorporating knotted cord. This provides an explicitly three-dimensional surface support for the written text and prioritises a haptic over an optic engagement with the work and a conceptual shift to opacity from transparency occurs. In doing so, specific aesthetic attention is drawn to the non-textual elements of support for the work. Much like Smithson's *Heap of Language* drawing which imagines words as lumps of geological material, the audience for *Essay with Knots* is encouraged not to read the text but to look at it as a physical thing that occupies space in the world. A similar effect of opacity is achieved with *Hostage Video Still with Time Stamp* (2005–2008). Here, Price uses images taken from the internet of the head of Nicholas Berg, the American Jewish freelance radio-tower repairman who was captured and then beheaded by Islamic militants in 2004. This was a notorious example of how images are circulated through online sources, in this case via a five-and-a-half-minute video which showed Berg first addressing the camera before being decapitated. Price used a low-resolution image of Berg's head, which was then printed on Mylar (a clear polyester film), thus transplanting the image from one medium to another. This arrests the image from its place in a restless flow of every changing content and gives it a fixed material form. But rather than offer up the image for scrutiny instead the primary content becomes the material support.

Writing on the work, David Joselit identified three modes in which the piece replicates the effects of dispersion: first, as a computer file which is copied until degradation; second, as the material of support such as the Mylar which is 'twisted or tied into crumpled configurations that serve as a spatial metaphor for the ostensibly "immaterial" traffic of images online'; and third, as 'the grisly and horrible physical violation of Berg is an explicitly biological form of "dispersion," in which a head is parted from its torso.'[15]

Folklore U.S.

Price's preoccupation with the material correlates to systems of dispersion is illustrated in Folklore U.S. The work was produced for dOCUMENTA (13) (2012) and comprised three closely related elements: a collection of paintings and fabric sculptures; a clothing line designed in collaboration with the fashion designer Tim Hamilton; and a fashion show. The respective venues in Kassel for each of these iterations were the Hauptbahnhof exhibition space; the commercial shop space of SinnLeffers where the clothes were on sale and in window displays; and the Folklore U.S. Spring/Summer 12 fashion show held in the Friedrichsplatz parking garage at the opening of dOCUMENTA (13). The main form shared across the paintings, sculptures and clothes was an envelope considered as both a container of material to be distributed and a symbol of business transactions. Both jackets and envelopes are the iconography of commerce, and both can conceal sensitive material. These forms were decorated by the corporate logos[16] and a crosshatched pattern.

In the choice of both form and content, Folklore U.S. evokes the iconography of the military-industrial-cultural complex of the United States. All of the work used the aesthetics of military clothing with the clothing line including a trench coat, a bomber, a flight suit and gaiters. Price has observed that there is a close link between military kit and sports and leisurewear exemplified in the bomber jacket as something designed for warfare that was subsequently appropriated as a fashionable item. This migration of materials and motifs from the military sphere to the public one also recalls Gillick's use of Plexiglas as a material used in both army equipment and corporate design and Steyerl's co-option of vocabularies and iconographies of surveillance. Price also insisted that only the techniques and resources of garment production be used in the production of the work saying:

> The final product is about the fabric, the trim, the cut. So even when a designer presents clothes within a narrative, like, "This is my hobo collection," or whatever, everyone watching the show is more concerned with the details of the clothes. What people are paying attention to is two buttons instead of three, or how the fabric drapes. The narrative information the designer supplies—"My collection is referencing 1930s haberdashery"—that's just historical footnotes, no one gets hung up on it. Whereas in the art world people can get very hung up on the concept, more so than on the material.[17]

This meant that if some process or material was not readily available, then it was not used. This effectively repositions Folklore U.S. within the systems of commerce and fashion signified by the use of the department store and fashion show as sites of display which repositions the piece outside of the system of the art world. As Price said (in conversation with Christopher Bollen):

> The project started as an experiment in fabrication, to make sculptures inside the world of garment design, inside its logic, and then to send the exact same materials and processes to Documenta through two separate channels: the art exhibition and the department store next to the Fridericianum. ... The point was to see how these languages warp the content in different ways, toward or away from critique, or use, or fashion, or readability.[18]

Positioning artworks within different systems of distribution provides an opportunity to observe the conditions of those different systems and the effects they have on the content that is dispersed amongst them. The difference between the domains of art and fashion is similar to what Dave Hickey observed as the difference between what he calls the Commercial Art World (CAW) and the Museum Art World (MAW). Hickey's point is that the Commercial Art World doesn't care about discourse or narrative history. It is not, in other words, engaged in questions of medium specificity or on any ontology of artworks. Instead, the main pre-occupations are judgements on what is, or isn't, relevant, 'in' or 'cool.'

The Stuff of Systems

Price gives material and, hence, aesthetic form to the flow of images and information that can seem to be, in everyday experience, dispersed, disembodied, dematerialised and merely virtual. He offers an answer to the question of whether the systems of dispersion can ever be grasped. Price clogs things up and arrests the flow of data with opaque, sticky and haptic matter.

This has relevance because it can sometimes feel that one can never properly see systems but only feel their effects. They are, after all, made of multiple, distributed parts dispersed throughout time and space. It makes no more sense, for example, to ask what the internet looks like than to think about how the global economic system smells. The global systems of everyday life are apparently ineffable, invisible and untouchable. This systemic turn is another way of thinking about modernity, that is those social, economic, technological and biological evolutions of the past few centuries. This move to systems is part of a fundamental, rapid, unstoppable and irreversible shift in how societies operate that Nicholas Negroponte called the move from 'atoms to bits.' Negroponte is referring to the migration of human interaction into virtual, distributed and cloud-like spaces. But, as he also observes, there is stuff left over. After all, he explains, it's your physical body that needs to go through the gate in an airport and 'when you go through customs you declare your atoms, not your bits.'[19]

It is often assumed that information is independent of the stuff through which it is communicated and that, as Negroponte says, 'A bit has no color, size, or weight, and it can travel at the speed of light. It is the smallest atomic element in the DNA of information.'[20] In other words, information treats the meanings of communication as independent of the means by which that information is communicated so that the message will be considered the same no matter what its material or mode of transmission might be, be that cables, sound or light. The dots and dashes of Morse Code, for example, can be transmitted through marks, beeps or flashes. What this ignores, however, is that each of these different materials and modes comes with different experiential effects. There are also tacit, second-hand meanings to communications, as well as their apparent messages. There is a phenomenology to communication that comes bundled in with its processes of coding and transmission.

This phenomenology of communication comes about by paying attention to the encounter with the quotidian elements that support and accompany messages. It is suggested by Paul Dourish's discussion on what he calls *The Stuff of Bits* from which this chapter borrows its title. As he points out the information that proliferates in contemporary society is only ever encountered in physical form: 'whether that is marks on a page, electrons flowing through wires, or magnetized segments of a spinning disk.'[21] Dourish observes, even though digital data is superficially composed of zeroes and ones, not all information is created equal:

> those 1s and 0s are not all equivalent or equally important. Some have greater significance than others. Some affect the others, some play more central roles in the representation, and some are more critical.[22]

Take, for example, a computer program. Whilst the operating system follows the instructions of the program, what the computer actually does is more than what is specified by the instructions. There are, for instance, different ways in which the functions of the program might be carried out that vary from computer to computer and between different operating systems. Different platforms have different means of working that may change how the program operates, which are not specifically detailed in the program itself. In other words, the experience of a computer program, and what it is like to use it, is not specifically designated by the set of instructions that it is comprised of. To type an essay using Microsoft Word on an Apple PowerBook is a different experience to using a Dell Latitude 7280, the laptop I am using to finish typing this text with its irritating and awkward keyboard.

These differences between systems hinge on the differences between the material manifestations of information as it is dispersed between systems. They lie in the gaps and nooks between what is coded and what is expressed; and between what is specified and what is subsequently produced. As Dourish observes, the mechanics and physicality of information processing are meaningful in themselves:

> In the slippage between notation and enaction, we find the lie of virtuality. The denial of materiality that is at the centre of virtuality rhetoric could be maintained only if the specification were complete: if a program really were an adequate account of what will happen in execution, if an mp3 really were a complete explanation of how music will be produced, or if a digital 3D model really specified what you'll see through a display. Yet, none of these are, in fact, the case.[23]

And it is precisely this slippage between notation and enaction within systems of dispersion and poking at the lie of virtuality that is what Price's work is, ultimately, about.

Notes

1 Seth Price, 'Dispersion,' in Beatrix Ruf & Axel Hochdörfer (eds.) *Social Synthetic* (Cologne: Koenig Books, 2017) pp. 67–85; pg. 71.
2 Beatrix Ruf and Axel Hochdörfer (eds.) *Social Synthetic* (Cologne: Koenig Books, 2017) pg. 334.

3 When asked about the act of using data as art, and whether this constituted a form of Institutional Critique of the systems related to art practices, Price replied: '*The hypocrisy would come from someone who thought I am condemning a system, or individuals, while benefiting from it, and I recognize that's a risk in making something like this. But I don't think of myself as a critical voice, in doing this. This is more like a self portrait.*' Seth Price, 'Organic Software: An Interview with Seth Price,' *Data Matters* (February 8th, 2018) emphasis added. Archived at: http://www.sethpricestudio.com/interviewarchive/OrgSoftInterview.pdf.

4 At http:// www.distributedhistory.com/Dispersion08.pdf. The first print publication was *The 25th Ljubljana Biennial of Graphic Arts*, ed. Christophe Cherix (Geneva: JRP Ringier, 2003) pg. 239.

5 Seth Price, 'Dispersion,' in Beatrix Ruf & Axel Hochdörfer (eds.) *Social Synthetic* (Cologne: Koenig Books, 2017) pp. 67–85.

6 Here, Price is invoking Art & Language. For example, Charles Harrison, "As to self-destruction: as Carles Guerra has observed, the work – and we don't just mean the artwork – is always *radically incomplete*. It tends to present itself as something cut-off - something potentially capable of re-absorption into the discourse, which may be of dialectical interest only in virtue of its effacement" Art & Language, 'Not Quite the Belaqua Pose – A Talk in Three Voices,' Published at: http://www.systemsart.org/index.html (accessed, June 2022) [emphasis added].

7 Seth Price, 'Dispersion,' in Beatrix Ruf & Axel Hochdörfer (eds.) *Social Synthetic* (Cologne: Koenig Books, 2017) pp. 67–85.

8 Seth Price, 'Dispersion,' in Beatrix Ruf & Axel Hochdörfer (eds.) *Social Synthetic* (Cologne: Koenig Books, 2017) pg. 71.

9 For example, it appears in the Social Synthetic version of the essay, cited here, but not in the version that appears in the catalogue for the group exhibition *Dispersion* curated by Polly Staple at the ICA, London (2008/2009).

10 Michael Newman has also suggested that the effect in film where the images are interrupted by the appearance of pouring liquid might be an allusion to Smithson's *Glue Pour* (1970).

11 Appearing in Arts of the Environment (ed. Kepes) and Arts Magazine respectively.

12 Robert Smithson, 'Spiral Jetty,' in Flam (ed.) *Robert Smithson: The Collected Writings* (Berkley: University of California Press, 1996) pg. 153.

13 Seth Price, 'Dispersion,' in Beatrix Ruf & Axel Hochdörfer (eds.) *Social Synthetic* (Cologne: Koenig Books, 2017) pp. 67–85.

14 Cited by Hochdörfer, pg. 25.

15 David Joselit, 'What to Do with Pictures,' *October*, 138 (2011) pp. 81–94, 84–85.

16 Capital One, The FDIC, Corbis, the ImageRights Agency. UBS. Paychex.

17 Seth Price, *Folklore U.S.* (London: Koenig Books: 2014), pg. 14.

18 Seth Price, *Folklore U.S.* (London: Koenig Books: 2014), pg. 14.

19 Nicholas Negroponte, *Being Digital* (New York: Alfred A. Knopf Inc., 1995) pg. 4.

20 Nicholas Negroponte, *Being Digital* (New York: Alfred A. Knopf Inc., 1995) pg. 14.

21 Paul Dourish, *The Stuff of Bits* (Cambridge: MIT Press, 2017) pg. 3.

22 Paul Dourish, *The Stuff of Bits* (Cambridge: MIT Press, 2017) pg. 17, original emphasis.

23 Paul Dourish, *The Stuff of Bits* (Cambridge: MIT Press, 2017) pp. 23–24.

References

Art & Language, 'Not Quite the Belaqua Pose – A Talk in Three Voices', Published at: http://www.systemsart.org/index.html (accessed June 2022)

Dourish, Paul, *The Stuff of Bits*, Cambridge: MIT Press, 2017

Joselit, David, 'What to Do with Pictures', *October*, 138 (2011) pp. 81–94

Negroponte, Nicholas, *Being Digital*, New York: Alfred A. Knopf Inc., 1995

Price, Seth, *Folklore U.S.*, London: Koenig Books, 2014

Price, Seth, 'Dispersion', in Beatrix Ruf & Axel Hochdörfer (eds.) *Social Synthetic* (pp. 66–80), Cologne: Koenig Books, 2017

Price, Seth, 'Organic Software: An Interview with Seth Price', *Data Matters* (February 8th, 2018) emphasis added. Archived at: http://www.sethpricestudio.com/interviewarchive/OrgSoftInterview.pdf

Ruf, Beatrix and Axel Hochdörfer (eds.) *Social Synthetic*, Cologne: Koenig Books, 2017

Smithson, Robert, 'Spiral Jetty', in Jack Flam (ed.) *Robert Smithson: The Collected Writings* (p. 153), Berkley: University of California Press, 1996.

3 Liam Gillick and the Aesthetics of Disappointment

The Age of Dispersion is characterised by the proliferation of systems. From health care systems to ecologies, political systems and economies, and industrial systems to the Internet, systems are ubiquitous and perhaps the dominant metaphor for how we organise and understand subjectivity today. This means that a contemporary artist is obliged to work with systems whether they choose to acknowledge this or not. In his engagement with systems, Liam Gillick both acknowledges and exemplifies these systemic conditions although, as I argue here, in doing so he does not celebrate them. Whilst there is some suggestion the works are underpinned by systems that run through and between them, they also seem to frustrate processes of communication and control. If there are systems at play in Gillick's work, then these systems are revealed to be uncommunicative, dysfunctional and, ultimately, disappointing. I argue here that it is precisely by virtue of this disappointment that the work has critical potential.

Superficially, at least, his work can often look systematic. It employs the grids, modular forms and iterative processes familiar from their use in Minimalist and Conceptual Art. In using the forms, colours and processes reminiscent of those of artists such as Sol LeWitt and Donald Judd Gillick appears to adopt the style and aesthetics of systems. In addition to this stylistic allusion to systems, Gillick uses a diverse range of social systems as platforms for distributing his practice including: publishing; education; architecture; design; and the art market.

In this second sense, he operates in the manner that Lane Relyea proposes typifies contemporary practice, that is, by using whatever platforms are available. Describing the move from medium to platform in contemporary practice, Relyea observes that the word comes from the discourses of engineering, design, management and advertising where it is used to describe some common element across diverse activities: '[P]latform denotes a basic, underlying architecture or system, a common workbench that, while itself stable and enduring, is open and flexible enough to allow for a high variety of interfaces, a range of inputs and outputs.'[1]

In such practices, which epitomise contemporary art, it becomes increasingly difficult to distinguish between artist, designer, entrepreneur and

DOI: 10.4324/9781003315322-4

celebrity as they all operate as cultural practitioners exploiting those systems that are at hand.

However, in both cases even though they give the superficial appearance of being operational, his use of systems be that stylistically or distributively is dysfunctional incomplete and imperfect. Hence, Gillick's art is, I argue, fundamentally *disappointing* by which I mean it doesn't require either aesthetic or conceptual contemplation. It is both aesthetically unsatisfactory and theoretically opaque. There is always something missing, incomplete or not fully resolved. Through this general attitude of incompleteness, Gillick's work gestures towards its reliance upon systems of distribution in the late capitalism in order to be presented as meaningful. But this meaning is never fully realised. And in doing so, his objects mimic the general conditions of subjectivity and its constitution via various systems of communication and control in the *Age of Dispersion.*

Diversity and Abstraction

The diversity and abstraction of the mediums and practices of Liam Gillick exemplify the conditions of contemporary art. He is a prolific collaborator working with curators, designers, architects, film-makers and others. This has included collaborating with Pringle under the brand, 'liamgillickforpringleof-scotland,' producing knitwear, bags and display structures for a pop-up store at Art Basel Miami Beach (2011); and constructing architectural interventions on the facades of buildings including The Home Office, London, *Home Office London (2002–05)* (2002–2005), and LAC, Lufthansa Aviation Centre, Frankfurt am Main, *Four Levels of Exchange* (2005). For *New Order + Liam Gillick: So it goes, ∑(No, 12k, Lg, 17Mif),* he worked with the band New Order at the Manchester International Festival to design the set for their performances in which the group deconstructed their back catalogue. As well as being an educator (professor at Columbia and Bard), he also writes extensively including regularly contributing to e-flux, an online journal, and producing books that merge fiction and theory including the anthology, *All Books.*[2] He represented Germany at the 53rd Venice Biennale with, *How Are You Going to Behave? A kitchen Cat Speaks* (2009), an installation comprising bare pine wood structures that recalled the functional domestic architecture of kitchens and workspaces; an animatronic cat; an abstract fable about the cat that could be heard being read out in the space; and a model of Arnold Bode's 1957 proposal for the new German Pavilion. He has even, as my closing example considers, been an actor in a major feature film.

As Sean Keller puts it:

> Here is an artist who wants to take it all on: global capitalism, corporate identity, product design, institutional critique, modernism and its aftermath, Minimalism and its aftermath, literary conventions, the linearity of time

itself…All of this is guided by an unresolved combination of the Marxist desire to explain everything with a single system (centered on economics) and a post-Marxist realization that no system can ever achieve this goal.[3]

Yet despite this diversity, one can normally spot a Gillick piece. His art has a recognisable style both in terms of a set of formal procedures he regularly employs, and a method of working. His signature pieces are modular forms made from aluminium frames, often including plexiglass, and coloured with powder-coated paint using standard processes of industrial production and the colour-matching system of the RAL Colour chart. A key characteristic of all his work, be they structures, texts, animations and so on, is that it points beyond its formal structure to a complex series of reference points to create a spirit of abstraction, obfuscation and dispersion. What, exactly, the work is doing and what the subject matter is remain mostly unclear and never resolved.

Consider, for example, *Denominator Platform*, a ceiling installation at Goethe-Institut Irland, Dublin (powder-coated aluminium, plexiglass 200 × 300 × 5 cm, 2018) (Figure 3.1).

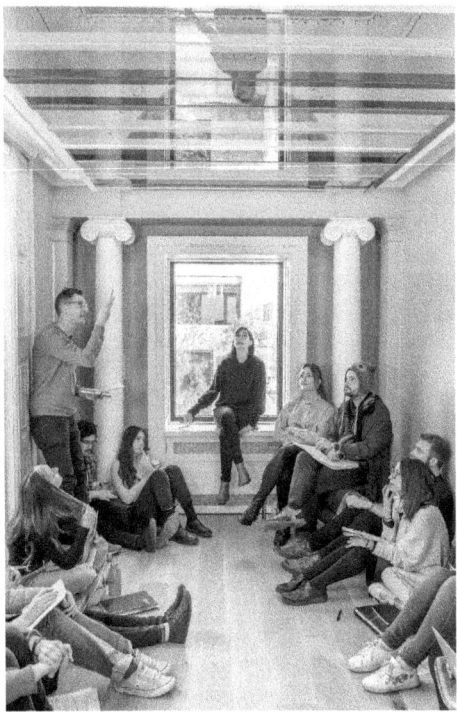

Figure 3.1 Liam Gillick: Denominator Platform (2017) at the Goethe Institut, Dublin

In formal terms, the work is a ceiling-mounted powder-coated aluminium frame of 2 by 3 metres holding rectangles of brightly coloured, transparent plexiglass. This piece was specially designed to be part of an educational collaboration between the Goethe-Institut and the MA/MFA Art in the Contemporary World at the National College of Art and Design, Ireland, under the title 'Common Denominator.'[4] The intention was for the platform to frame and contextualise a program of education events involving the artist, the course team and a group of postgraduate students. It activated the space underneath itself by designating it as a site of consideration and aesthetic reflection. But it also withdraws from that very space by virtue of being discrete and modest. It is a simple and non-complex form that doesn't reward sustained reflection. When operating as the site for discussion, it fades from view.

Positioned at the meeting point of education, design and art and as an injunction to discussion, *Denominator Platform* sits alongside several pieces by Gillick with 'discussion' in the title. These include several very similar structures with titles such as *Discussion Platform* and *Discussion Island*.

As with much of Gillick's work, the materials of the platforms and the islands follow the logic of corporate design with use of powder-coated, machine-formed aluminium, Plexiglas and the reiteration of modular elements. As Gillick observed: 'Plexiglass and aluminium are the materials of renovation and refurbishment. They are the materials of McDonald's signs, and display cases in Prada, of aeroplanes and bullet-proof screens in banks, of really sexy nightclub floors and riot shields.'[5]

The work often alludes to standard processes of mechanical engineering. In particular, Gillick is drawing on his extensive research into processes of automobile production, such as the Kalmar plant in Sweden, which produced cars for Volvo between 1974 and 1994. As he states, here one can find a model of how social systems in general operate in a post-Fordist context.[6]

On *Discussion Platforms*, it is worth quoting Gillick's description in full as it articulates the deadpan nature of both their articulation and their formal qualities:

The works consist of an aluminium framework, either anodised or plain, filled with cross beams of aluminium with the resulting framework filled with Plexiglas, wood or other panelling. The platforms are usually fixed to one or more walls. In at least one case the platform hangs from the ceiling without touching any walls. The weight of the cantilevered platforms is either stressed through cables running up to the ceiling or through the supporting poles running up from the floor. It is extremely important at all times to maintain a standard relationship between the platform and supports. The best way for the work to hang is with straight cables running directly down from the ceiling, never running at an angle and definitely never running at an acute angle back to the wall. The reason for this is that the standard installation offers a low level of tension to the platform, if the cables run at angles then a sprung tension is established in the platform that can result in distortion of the work and in extreme case total collapse of the work. Trust me, I've tried it.[7]

This seems to be saying a lot whilst not communicating much and this infuses the work with a general spirit of abstraction and awkwardness. They seem simple, but don't offer up a simple interpretation or meaning. Gillick, in discussion with Beatrix Ruff, described this awkwardness in relation to his *Discussion Platform* pieces:

People either functionalise the work, instrumentalise it, or use it as a metaphorical structure. The truth is that the work is none of these things alone. The object is neither just functional nor is it exactly a metaphor of the idea of place for something to happen. It has potential, it is in a constant state of 'becoming.'[8]

Gillick's use of corporate materials and iconography is repeated in the text *Discussion Island/Big Conference Centre*[9] produced to accompany a *Discussion Island* installation. This story is abstracted and fragmented, and it is hard to follow a clear narrative. As it describes itself, it is a text that:

sweeps across various locations and situations in order to create a complex picture of how decisions are made at a point where there is no strong shared ideological consensus about how the future should be... DISCUSSION ISLAND starts in the new big conference centre of the title. A large space has gone unplanned and unnoticed in the new building in order to create a crisis, which will permit some degree of freedom within the planned structure.[10]

Given that *Discussion Island* is comprised of multiple elements, the primary focus of the work, (be that aesthetically or conceptually) is ambiguous. This was a stated intention for the work, and he claimed: 'With this book the artworks related to it occurred both before and after the writing of the text and in many cases set the scene for a text that had few clear locations.'[11]

This strategy of deferral of aesthetic and conceptual focus *Discussion Island,* as previously argued for Seth Price's work, recalls Smithson's concept of the Site/Non-Site. It is constantly referring back to itself as a complex, recursive and yet never fully intuitable system of interconnected elements. As Roberts observes:

Gillick's visual and sculptural production therefore ought not to be taken to stand for his practice as a whole. It is, instead, a part of a more complex constellation of elements, which has the effect of relativizing the apparent claims of sculpture itself.[12]

Gillick's discourse is prolific but prolix and partial. It frequently refers to his objects tangentially. Consider this passage for example which accompanied his contribution to the German Pavilion at the Venice Biennale (2009):

> There will be a cat that can speak. All the people of the town will be very proud of their speaking cat. People will come every day to hear what it has to say. It will be very cynical but never mean. It will see everything and understand it all. After a while people will only come on the weekends or drop by on the way home from work or school. ... It will take a deep surreptitious suck of the children's breath and as they reel and swoon, glide and dream it will begin to tell them a true story about the wisdom of a kitchen cat....[13]

What exactly this might mean is unclear, and it does not help in unpacking the formal elements of the installation. And whilst the objects Gillick produces might be read as merely what Lütticken calls: 'quasi-illustrations of his discourse,'[14] any clear correspondence between text and object is obscured or frustrated. Gillick acknowledges this process of deferral in his somewhat cryptic claims for one of the works:

> By leaving the first platform – (THE WHAT IF? SCENARIO) SECOND STAGE DISCUSSION PLATFORM AND SURFACE DESIGN, 1996 – alone in a room with nothing else and no other explanation, I was hoping to indicate that there was a revision of ideas and a visual shift about to take place. It functioned as an abstracted discussion space designating a move away from a text heavy, dinner party history play into attempts to look at the conditions around the planned middle ground. It echoed those sociopolitical spaces which are fought over within a neo-liberal consensus.[15]

In the face of this deferral, Gillick makes objects and performs gestures that look like and perform the role of art. They are the tokens that give him access to a number of different systems of distribution and display, circulating in the economic and institutional systems that form the support structure for contemporary art, such as the market, museums, galleries, biennales and art fairs. Gillick's objects become instances of communication that give him access to the various systems that he operates within and that his work is dispersed throughout. However, rather than being entirely complicit with such systems, Gillick presents a discursive engagement with them, in order to 'confront a socio-economic system that bases its growth and collapse upon "projections."'[16] Yet whilst doing so, they also disrupt and disappoint those systems and render their communications ambiguous.

Thus, Gillick engages in an aesthetics of systems in a different mode to that of seriality. He invokes systems to challenge the autonomy of both the art object and the process of authorship by demonstrating that, whilst inanimate, these objects are dispersed throughout different systems of communication and control and require these systems to frame and articulate their identity. These systems include the galleries, art fairs and exhibitions where the objects are shown; economic systems in which they appear as commodities; and the discursive systems of contemporary criticism and art history where they circulate as dispersed discursive objects. Yet, these objects are also, crucially, not entirely reducible to such systems. They also disrupt them through strategies of contradiction and obfuscation, and, as Gillick states, *failure*:

> The abstract draws artists towards itself as a semi-autonomous zone just out of reach. It produces the illusion of a series of havens and places that might reduce the contingent everyday to a sequence of distant inconveniences. It is the concretisation of the abstract into a **series of failed forms** that lures the artist into repeated attempts to "create" the abstract–fully aware that this very act produces things that are the representation of impossibilities. In the current context this means that the abstract is a realm of denial and deferment–a continual reminder to various publics that varied acts of art has taken place and the authors were probably artists.[17]

Conclusion

In the feature film *Exhibition* (Joanna Hogg, UK, 2014), Gillick plays what is plausibly a version of himself; the role of a conceptual artist living with his partner in a modernist house in North London. Neither Gillick nor his co-star, the musician Viv Albertine are professional actors, and his performance is naturalistic. His filmic presence is deadpan, downbeat and somewhat inscrutable; it is disrupting and deflationary. In the film, Gillick appears to be acting in much the same way that his objects perform in other exhibitionary contexts, that is through a certain difficult to read obstinacy. His body, like his objects, presents some disruption to a system of communication. Gillick admitted that he gave Hogg 'a hard time. Not giving someone their line. Having my back to the camera. Just playing.' He describes the process thus:

> Although we had no time between her request and the start of the shoot, she did suggest that I look at Bresson's Notes on Cinema before the shooting started. He writes about the actor as mannequin. I decided to take this route. I often cleared my mind completely before scenes and just played them as a body in space. Sometimes I didn't even listen to the other actors around me – just sensed myself in space. I didn't think my character would be a good listener so I played him as someone aware of his body who doesn't hear everything first time—who is hearing everything for the first time—and mishearing some of it.[18]

Here, Gillick is describing his approach to acting as being a body that doesn't communicate well and which interacts only awkwardly with its environment and other actors. My argument is that this is an apt description of how all his work in general responds to the environments and systems it is positioned within. Through the use of modular and iterative processes, Gillick generates new systems within his own oeuvre. Despite the superficial appearance of being operational and communicative, his systems are incomplete, imperfect, dysfunctional and disappointing. His art does not offer a satisfactory aesthetic experience, but rather frustrates sustained contemplation and attempts to understand, enjoy or like it.

Through this disappointment, Gillick alienates us from the systems he deploys. Our attention is drawn away from the art objects towards the systems they sit within and, consequently, to our position within and reliance upon the contemporary systems of communication and control. In doing so, Gillick's systems also present an aesthetic analogue for the contingent and dispersed conditions of subjectivity in the *Age of Dispersion*. Through strategies of abstraction and deflation, Gillick's work is doubly disappointing: it frustrates any expectations of immersive spectacle in the face of the industries of entertainment and culture, whilst it also frustrates the supposedly radical antagonistic gestures of those avant-garde practices that were historically opposed to such spectacle. Gillick neither valorises nor attacks systems but rather presents something more deflationary, and in doing so, provides an opportunity to engage in a critique of two systems: the system of capital and the system of art and point to their mutual complicity in the production of dispersed subjectivity.

Notes

1 Lane Relyea, *Your Everyday Art World* (Cambridge: MIT Press, 2013) pg. 20.

2 Liam Gillick: (i) *Proxemics; Selected Writings (1988–2006)* (Zurich: JRP|Ringier, 2007); (ii) *All Books* (London: Book Works, 2009); (iii) *Industry and Intelligence: Contemporary Art since 1820* (New York: Columbia University Press, 2016).

3 Sean Keller, 'Liam Gillick, Museum of Contemporary Art, Chicago,' *Artforum* (April 2010).

4 The course team are Francis Halsall, Declan Long, Sarah Pierce. From the press release:

> The 'Common Denominator,' programme has its origin in the writings of Bauhaus architect Walter Gropius, who made a case for identifying the core qualities defining a particular style, or the principles from which new forms of building, and teaching, might progress. The 'Common Denominator' programme at NCAD takes Gropius's term as a starting point for reflecting on varieties and possibilities of commonality today. Through exhibitions, seminars, discussions and more, it interrogates what it might mean now to speak of political solidarity, civic standards or even aesthetic values. We will consider – as Gropius sought to do – the relationship between common commitments and necessary possibilities of individual belief, expression and action.

5 Sean O'Hagan, 'This Is Not An Art Gallery,' *The Observer* (Sunday 5th May, 2002) at: https://www.theguardian.com/education/2002/may/05/arts.highereducation (accessed, 20th February 2019).

6 Liam Gillick, 'Maybe It Would be Better if We Worked in Groups of 3?" *E-Flux Journal*, (2009) http://www.e-flux.com/journal/maybe-it-would-be-better-if-we-worked-in-groups-of-three-part-1-of-2-the-discursive/ (accessed, 26th February 2019).

7 Liam Gillick, in Robert Fleck (ed.) *Exhibition Catalogue for Ein Langer Spaziergang… Zwei kurze Stege* (Köln: Snoeck, 2010), pg. 173.

8 John Baldessari et al., *Again the Metaphor Problem and Other Engaged Critical Discourses About Art. A Conversation between John Baldessari, Liam Gillick and Lawrence Weiner, Moderated by Beatrix Ruff* (New York, Wein: Springer, 2007) pg. 24.

9 Liam Gillick, *Discussion Island/Big Conference Centre* (Kunstverein Ludwigsberg/ Orchard Gallery Derry, 1997) republished in Liam Gillick, *All Books* (London: Book Works, 2009).

10 In Liam Gillick, *All Books* (London: Book Works, 2009) pg. 140.

11 In Liam Gillick, *All Books* (London: Book Works, 2009) pg. 140.

12 Bill Roberts, 'Burnout: Liam Gillick's Post-Fordist Aesthetics,' *Art History* 36(1) (February 2013) pp. 180–205; 201.

13 Liam Gillick, 'A Kitchen Cat Speaks' available at: http://www.liamgillick.info/home/texts/a-kitchen-cat-speaks (accessed, 20th February 2019).

14 In Monika Szewczyk et al. (eds) *Meaning Liam* Gillick (Cambridge: The MIT Press, 2009) pg. 40.

15 Liam Gillick and Anthony Spira, 'Speculation and Planning,' in Liam Gillick, *The Wood Way* (London: The Whitechapel Art Gallery, 2002). pp. 14–18/15.

16 Liam Gillick, 'Berlin Statement' (Hamburger Banhof, Feb 12th, 2009).

17 Liam Gillick, 'Abstract' (2011) originally commissioned by Museo Tamayo in Mexico City for the exhibition reader Microhistorias y macromundos, volume 3, as part of the exhibition Abstracción posible/Abstract Possible. Available at: http://www.on-curating.org/issue-20-reader/abstract.html#.XHgWeMD7R0w [Emphasis added].

18 https://archive.ica.art/bulletin/exhibition-interview-liam-gillick.

References

Baldessari, John, et al., *Again the Metaphor Problem and Other Engaged Critical Discourses About Art. A Conversation between John Baldessari, Liam Gillick and Lawrence Weiner, Moderated by Beatrix Ruff*, New York, Wien: Springer, 2007

Gillick, Liam, 'A Kitchen Cat Speaks', available at: http://www.liamgillick.info/home/texts/a-kitchen-cat-speaks (accessed, 20th July 2022)

Gillick, Liam, *The Wood Way*, London: The Whitechapel Art Gallery, 2002

Gillick, Liam, *Proxemics; Selected Writings (1988–2006)*, Zurich: JRP|Ringier, 2007

Gillick, Liam, 'Berlin Statement', Hamburger Bahnhof, Feb 12th, 2009

Gillick, Liam, *Discussion Island/Big Conference Centre*, Kunstverein Ludwigsburg/ Orchard Gallery Derry, 1997, republished in Gillick, Liam, *All Books*, London: Book Works, 2009

Gillick, Liam and Spira, Anthony, 'Speculation and Planning', in Liam Gillick (ed.) *The Wood Way* (pp. 14–18/15), London: The Whitechapel Art Gallery, 2002.

Gillick, Liam, *All Books*, London: Book Works, 2009

Gillick, Liam, 'Maybe It Would be Better if We Worked in Groups of 3?', *E-Flux Journal*, (2009) http://www.e-flux.com/journal/maybe-it-would-be-better-if-we-worked-in-groups-of-three-part-1-of-2-the-discursive/ (accessed, 22nd July 2022)

Gillick, Liam, 'Installation Instructions, 1998' in Robert Fleck (ed.) *Exhibition Catalogue for Ein Langer Spaziergang... Zwei kurze Stege* (p. 173), Köln: Snoeck, 2010

Gillick, Liam, *Industry and Intelligence: Contemporary Art since 1820*, New York: Columbia University Press, 2016

Keller, Sean, 'Liam Gillick, Museum of Contemporary Art, Chicago', *Artforum* (April 2010)

O'Hagan, Sean, 'This Is Not an Art Gallery', *The Observer* (Sunday 5th May, 2002) at: https://www.theguardian.com/education/2002/may/05/arts.highereducation (accessed, 20th February 2019)

Relyea, Lane, *Your Everyday Art World*, Cambridge: MIT Press, 2013

Roberts, Bill, 'Burnout: Liam Gillick's Post-Fordist Aesthetics', *Art History* 36(1) (February, 2013) pp 180–205

Szewczyk, Monika, et al. (eds) *Meaning Liam Gillick*, Cambridge: The MIT Press, 2009

4 Martin Creed, the Anti-Readymade and the Dispersed Art Object

Martin Creed's most well-known work is a room where a light goes on and off. *Work No. 227: The lights going on and off* (2000) was his contribution to the Turner Prize exhibition the year he won. It is exemplary of both Creed's work in particular and contemporary art in general. It is at once incredibly simple yet complex; commonplace and exceptional; and both banal and beautiful. In activating these contradictions, Creed gives us an example of how art may become totally dispersed into its environment. In doing so, it pivots aesthetic attention away from discreet art objects onto an embodied, multisensory and *dispersed* subject engaging in the textures of the world.

His artworks have included very simple, minimal gestures including crumpled balls of paper, unadorned stacks of plywood and a piece of blu-tack with an impression of a finger. He's made short films of people defecating and making themselves vomit and also produces music in the form of a paredback form of low-fi pop/punk that typically uses a very few basic chords, repetition and simple lyrics, such as *Thinking/Not Thinking* (2011), which repeats the phrase 'I was thinking and then I was not thinking' over a two-chord riff (a chord for each state) for about two minutes. He describes his process as a taking-away of things: 'I think: I've got to try and clear away the shit and try and make something that is simple and direct, and not at all complicated.'[1]

It is easy to attribute such engagement with, and appropriation of, everyday subject matter and materials as being anti-aesthetic.[2] However, as I argue here, rather than being either Minimalist or anti-aesthetic, Creed's practice is the opposite in being both *maximalist* and an injunction to treat everything as an object of aesthetic reflection. Hence, in much the same manner that Seth Price explored the other side of the coin of conceptualism, namely, materialisation, Creed investigates the aesthetic textures of everyday life rather than the anti-aesthetic (conceptual) qualities of art.

In claiming this, I argue that Creed's work be considered as the structural equivalent but inverse of the Readymade. His things are Anti-Readymades. That is, far from being anti-aesthetic, Creed's objects provide a means of rethinking our encounters with all objects in the world in aesthetic terms regardless of whether they are art or not. Thus, this chapter uses Creed's work to argue that

DOI: 10.4324/9781003315322-5

his work is a form of address to embodied subjectivity that has a particular resonance today as a means of mobilising art practices as philosophically significant. In doing so, Creed retains the essentially modernist autonomy of aesthetic experience, but does so in such a manner that this experience is uncoupled from a particular category of objects (art) and applied more generally to objects of experience. In other words, Creed shows how art in general can be a practice in which objects are constructed that are complex and relational and *dispersed*.

Creed's Maximalism

Creed seems to consider anything in the world as both potential medium and subject matter. As a result, it is also, as is outlined below, bursting at the seams with art historical references.

In 2012, Martin Creed staged the enormously ambitious *London 2012 Work No. 1197: All the Bells* (2012).[3] The work was conceived for the 2012 London Olympics with the description 'All the bells in a country rung as quickly and as loudly as possible for three minutes.'[4] At 8:12am, bells were rung all over Britain and included church bells, handbells, doorbells and Big Ben at the Palace of Westminster along with the bells in the national assemblies in Scotland, Wales and Northern Ireland. On several counts, this was a complicated work. It was administratively intricate, for example, involving Big Ben tolling outside of its schedule for the first time since 1952; it involved the coordination of a large number of people and was spatially diffuse. It was diverse stylistically too with each bell playing a different melody, tone and rhythm. The medium of the work is intricate and unfixed too involving not a single, discreet and simple object but multiple actors and elements including sound, performance, site-specific locations, broadcast media (the bells appeared on BBC radio and Channel 4) and various forms of documentation.

Given the complexity of *Work No. 1197*, it is unsatisfactory to refer to the work as minimal in stylistic terms. It is certainly not minimalist in the terms identified by Barbara Rose in her landmark essay 'ABC Art' in 1965, which gave the definition of a type of art that was:

> stripped to its bare, irreducible minimum... in its severe, reduced simplicity, or in its frequent kinship to the world of things... The concept of 'Minimal Art' which is surely applicable to the empty, repetitious, uninflected art of many young painters, sculptors, dancers, and composers working now.[5]

Typically, Minimalist art is non-representational, with no surface ornament and no apparent expressive content. Barbara Rose observed:

> That these young artists attempt to suppress or withdraw content from their works is undeniable. That they wish to make art that is as bland, neutral and as redundant as possible also seems clear. The content, then, if we are

to take the work at face value, should be nothing more than the total of the series of assertions that it is this or that shape and takes up so much space and is painted such a colour and made of such a material.[6]

This attitude is exemplified in one Minimalist artist Carl Andre observing another, Frank Stella's stripe paintings such as *The Marriage of Reason and Squalor II* (1959):

> Art excludes the unnecessary. Frank Stella has found it necessary to paint stripes. There is nothing else in his painting. Frank Stella is not interested in expression or sensitivity... Frank Stella's painting is not symbolic. His stripes are the paths of brush on canvas. These paths lead only into painting.[7]

This view on subject matter was corroborated by Stella who stated of his work in 1964 that 'What you see is What you See (and nothing more)'[8] and that: 'all I want anyone to get out of my paintings, and all I ever get out of them, is the fact that you can see the whole idea without any confusion.'[9]

Such strategies are also present in Creed's use of repetition such as in *524* (2006), which is a series of eight simple, oblique, parallel red lines made by a marker pen on A4 paper or his stacks of plywood such as *571* (2006) [252 ×185 × 252 cm] and *1017* (2009) [182 × 91 × 182 cm]. All of these works have the appearance that a simple mathematical principle regulates the whole compositional schema. This is to say that they are also balanced in terms of composition elements. There is no aesthetic hierarchy within the work. No prominence is given to any specific aspect of the work. And an outcome of this is that the work is taken as a single, that is to say, simple compositional unit.

However, despite the superficial resemblance to Minimalism, Creed's work often seems to be the result of an attempt to cram as much of life and the world into the experience of art. This is one interpretation of his phrase, 'the whole world + the work = the whole world,' which is reiterated in several of his works; namely, that the world already contains the work of art, and the work of art contains the whole world. Hence, instead of gestures of severe, reduced simplicity, Creed's work instead might be characterised as maximalist rather than minimalist. Creed has described his attraction to art as: 'I did art because I thought it had all the other things in it; it seemed like the field called art contained everything else.'[10] In doing so, Creed is exemplary of contemporary artistic practices of *dispersion*. As the all examples here illustrate, contemporary artists can use anything as their mediums, use anything as their subject matter and the means of production available to them is similarly multiple and open-ended.

This diversity of materials and promiscuity of methods has two implications for the general argument of this book and for the particular consideration of what Creed does: first, that any modernist gap between art and life has become irrevocably eroded. And second, as a direct result, art is now thoroughly dispersed throughout, and hence aesthetically inseparable from, the social systems of their support.

Creed's diversity and promiscuity manifests in the multiple art historical references that can be made in his work. This includes stylistic similarities such as the use of iterative procedures prevalent in Minimalism and the use of repeated lines used frequently by Creed (in drawings and wall pieces) recalling similar gestures by Agnes Martin and Robert Ryman. His repeated use of wood in stacks (e.g. *Work No. 841 Plywood* (2007)) might recall Carl Andre's multiple use of cedar (e.g. *Cedar Piece* (1964)), and Creed's use of neon to make wall-based text works such as *Work No. 988 EVERYTHING IS GOING TO BE ALRIGHT* (2009) recalls the extensive use of it in conceptual practices most notably by Bruce Nauman. He has made several films involving unflinching scrutiny of bodily process including *Work No. 610 Sick Film* (2006), a 21-minute film showing people making themselves vomit; *Work No. 200* (2006), which for one minute 18 seconds, a person with their back to the camera squats and defecates onto the floor; and *Work No. 730* (2007), which is a four-minute, ten-second shot from a single, fixed camera of a slow motion close-up of a penis sliding between buttocks. Such a dispassionate presentation of visceral bodily activities calls to mind similar treatments in experimental films such as Andy Warhol's *Blow Job* (1964), a film of the titular sex act, or Bruce Nauman's *Bouncing Balls* (1969), which is a close-up of testicles being bounced up and down; or extreme attempts to push a body, as an artistic medium, to a limit or point of breakdown seen in the work of Vito Aconcci (*Three Adaption Studies* (1970)) or Chris Burden (*Shoot* (1971))

Arte Povera is another obvious reference. The Italian movement was named by Germano Celant in 1967 to refer to art that was poor or impoverished and which expressed in the use of non-traditional materials such as Untitled (1968) (also known as *Eating Structure*) by Giovanni Anselmo in which a small block of granite is bound by a copper wire to the side of a larger, upright block of granite with a lettuce between the two. This means that if the lettuce dries out and shrinks, the smaller stone will drop, hence requiring the sculpture to be replenished with lettuces. Creed has also made work with simple everyday materials including balls of crumpled paper, *Work No 125, A sheet of paper crumpled into a* ball (1995) and assortments of balls of various shapes, colours and materials, such as in *Work No. 457* (2005). In Alighiero Boetti *Yearly Lamp* (1966), a light bulb in a wooden box turns on randomly for 11 seconds each year, which has a direct resonance with Creed's *The lights going on and off*, which has had several iterations as *Work No. 127* (1995); *Work No. 160* (1996); and *Work No. 227* (2000). In Jannis Kounellis' *Untitled (12 horses)* (1969), 12 live horses were installed in the L'Attico Gallery in Rome. Creed repeated Kounellis' gesture of occupying a gallery space with living entities in *Work No. 850* (2008) in which runners ran as fast as they could for 30 seconds through Tate Britain followed by a 30-second pause.

Other reference points might include Conceptual art. Consider, for example, *Work No. 91 One Packet of Blue Tack* (1994–2001), which consists of instructions including to: 'stick blobs of Blu-Tack to walls and surfaces throughout the space [...] Locate blobs wherever you like, ensuring only that there is at least one in each room (including toilets, office etc).' This recalls works such as Yoko Ono's Instruction Pieces such as the 'instruction painting' *Voice Piece for Soprano* (1961) comprising the instructions: 'Scream. 1. against the wind 2. against the wall 3. against the sky' or Robert Barry's sparse textual pieces such as *All the things I know but of which I am not at the moment thinking – 1:36 pm. June 15, 1969* (1969), which is installed as a pencil text on a wall. Sol LeWitt's *Wall Drawings* (1,200 created between 1968 and 2007) are also invoked through both their initial manifestation as instructions and in the stylistic similarity between them and Creed's works such as *Work No 840* (2007), which was shown at the Douglas Hyde Gallery, Dublin, as a simple lattice pattern of diagonal, parallel stripes, 23cm wide, of yellow emulsion painted on the entire back wall of the gallery.

If Creed's work is crammed with connections to art historical practices of art after modernism, then this exemplifies the general condition of contemporary art made in the inescapable shadow of the Readymade and the seeming redundancy of originality in the condition of the end of art. Massimiliano Gioni observes that Creed's pieces are akin to musical scores that can be repeated: 'Creed doesn't believe in originality, the unique, the eccentric. Instead, he is fascinated by quantity and repetition. The system is more important than its individual parts.'[11]

The system that Gioni refers to is doubled in Creed's work: first, internally, through the repetitive, systemic gestures he employs throughout his work and second, through the connections which inevitably refer the work to a system of art historical precedents and references.[12]

Anti: the Anti-Aesthetic

Creed's Maximalism puts his practice (much like Seth Price and Theaster Gates) at odds with the dominant art historical paradigms that trace their genealogies from the anti-aesthetic legacy of Duchamp such as Minimalism, conceptualism and Institutional Critique.

A definition of Minimalism, for instance, was given in 1965 by the philosopher Richard Wollheim when he identified Minimal Art as art, which met the 'minimum criteria,' of being art. This applied both to work in the tradition of Duchamp's Readymades and the simple, iterative gestures of Minimalism. The legacy of the Readymade is often identified with scepticism towards, if not a deliberate subversion of, the aesthetic content of the works of art.

A consequence of this general move from the prioritising of the visual content of the work as its primary subject matter is a move away from modernism in general, which is usually traced back to Duchamp's famous hatred of 'retinal art,' in favour of the 'non-retinal beauty of grey matter.'[13] Bound up with this was Duchamp's attempt to sideline aesthetics in his work in favour of an aesthetic approach. That is, rather than be anti-aesthetic, he preferred to consider his work as not concerned with aesthetics at all. For Arthur Danto, this condition was exemplified by work such as Andy Warhol's *Brillo Box* (1964), which was famously used in his formulation of what became subsequently known as the Institutional Theory of Art. Danto claimed that as phenomena, these objects were indistinguishable from mere things yet were ensured their status as art by virtue of being in an institutional setting.[14]

Danto argues that to appreciate something as a work of art is to acknowledge its situation relative to the Artworld. The Artworld provides the context and necessary conditions under which art is received and encountered. Thus, one's knowledge of the work of art (such as artistic intention, historical references and style) actively informs and generates the context of the work of art. Danto's test cases such as Warhols's *Brillo-Box* (1964), a plywood replica of commercial packaging, are 'paired cases where only one member of the couple is an artwork.'[15]

Such examples of self-similar objects are used to demonstrate that one cannot use perceptual and aesthetic qualities as a means of making distinctions between art and non-art:

> we cannot appeal to aesthetic considerations in order to get our definition of art, inasmuch as we need the definition of art in order to identify the sorts of aesthetic responses appropriate to works of art in contrast with mere things.[16]

The Readymade, on the one hand, is an appropriation of something that was not art such as in Rauschenberg, *Bed* (1955), a bed covered in expressionistic paint marks and mounted on the wall. Creed has frequently used prefabricated and readymade objects in his practice including metronomes, *Work No. 233* (1999), a selection of balls of different colours and sizes, *Work No. 370* (2004) and his well-known and frequent installations where a room is filled with balloons such as *Work No. 628* (2007).

On the other hand, because of the process of appropriation, there is what John Roberts refers to as the 'Displacement' of authorship[17] and the removal of artistic craft in the process of creation. For example, after 1964 Judd stopped making his own sculptures and passed the task over the task to an engineer; just as Duchamp himself had his own Readymades remade as multiples in 1964. Creed, too, uses industrial processes of mass production to produce his works such as in pieces using the phrase 'the whole world + the work = the whole world,' which has been made as a billboard installed in London, *Work No. 143b* (1998), a neon installation on the façade of Tate Britain, *Work No. 232* (2000) as well as other published and installed iterations of pieces featuring those words. However, despite these and the other similarities to a myriad of practices that I've introduced above, Creed's work, I argue, is on an adjacent trajectory to the familiar art historical narratives of art after modernism.

Conclusion

There is an obvious preoccupation with visceral experience in Creed's work be that in the bodily actions of running, puking, shitting or fucking or the direct address to spectators presented in his performances and environments of occupied rooms. In the absence of apparent representational, conceptual or metaphorical content for these examples the visceral experience emerges as the primary content of the work. This is the generosity of Creed's art. It directs attention away from itself and gifts that attention back onto the spectator. It allows them to experience their own experiences without art or artists getting in the way of those experiences. This, I think, is both the meaning and munificence of his notorious *Work No. 227: The lights going on and off* (2000). It offers an experience that anyone can grasp regardless of their art historical knowledge, level of concentration or taste. It is almost not there and almost not art.

I conclude with an anecdote from a few years ago concerning a visit with students to a Martin Creed exhibition at the Douglas Hyde gallery in Trinity College Dublin. The show included *Work # 701 nails* (2007), which is seven nails of varying lengths stuck into the wall alongside drawings, wall paintings and a plywood stack (*Work No. 841 Plywood* (2007)). They found the work unsatisfactory, and some reactions were downright hostile. When asked why, the responses given were surprising for students studying and practicing art in the 21st century if only because they repeated criticisms of art that could have been made 200 years previously, as if modernism had never occurred. It triggered a series of damning connoisseurial judgements. They included complaints that the work was unoriginal, unskilfully produced and was conceptually unsophisticated and that it wasn't aesthetically pleasing. In a later discussion, it seemed that it wasn't the works' formal qualities that had provoked such judgements but rather its situation within an art gallery in the 21st century. One student explained that if they encountered a work like the plywood stack in a non-art context (in the square at the back of the art school, for instance), it could be 'fascinating' and 'intriguing' as an interplay of textures and provide a rich perceptual and aesthetic experience. Thus, as far as these students were concerned Creed's work failed within the specific context of an art institution (which bears with it an inheritance of a multitude of historical precedents). In other words, in an inversion of Danto's argument in *The Transfiguration of the Commonplace* that we need to establish whether something is a work of art before, we ascertain whether we can have an aesthetic experience of it, when Creed's work is viewed *as art* it failed. Yet when viewed as part of everyday experience, by strategically forgetting that it was art, Creed's work offered the potential for aesthetic experience.

Such strategic forgetting that these objects are art provides the opportunity to view the work in a manner that recalls Clement Greenberg's often caricatured, arch-modernist claim that 'the purely plastic or abstract qualities of the work are the only ones that count.'[18] This repeats the modernist commitment to the autonomy of aesthetic experience whilst, crucially, separating this experience from particular objects (art) and applying it to a phenomenon in general. Such a turn away from art means attempting to experience the work outside of an art historical frame, that is in an art historically neutral way. This offers the dual promise of an aesthetic experience that isn't mediated by expectations as to the effects that a particular work of art should produce; and uncoupling aesthetic experiences from the institutional power structures of the systems of art. It means approaching Creed's work as if all the obvious anti- and post-modernist precedents for it could all be forgotten. Creed seemed to be alluding to this amnesia when asked whether he would define what he does as art:

> Not necessarily no ... No! ...No! it's just stuff... extra stuff in the world... it can be good or bad stuff... but I don't call it 'art' because I don't find that useful... I don't find it useful to think about art.[19]

By disavowing the obvious, inescapable art historical references, Creed redirects attention away from the work and its place in a system of art historical references, and back onto the world his authored objects sit within. Such forgetting grants spectators the opportunity to forget that they're looking at art. This is exemplified in *Work No. 1059 The Scotsman Steps* (2010) where Creed worked with the somewhat grotty enclosed public staircase in Edinburgh leading from the train station to the Royal Mile and covered each step in a different coloured marble. To the frequent users of the steps, the work is invisible, unless they take the time to pay attention to their surroundings and their place within them. The work embodies his statement that 'The Whole Work + The Work = The Whole World.' He has said of them that 'stepping on the different marble steps is like walking through the world.'[20]

In the Scotsman Steps work, as for all Creed's practice, certain historical precedents and certain expectations for the work can be bracketed in order to focus aesthetic attention on the interesting perceptual effects of everyday experience without worrying about the bother of art getting in the way (Figure 4.1).

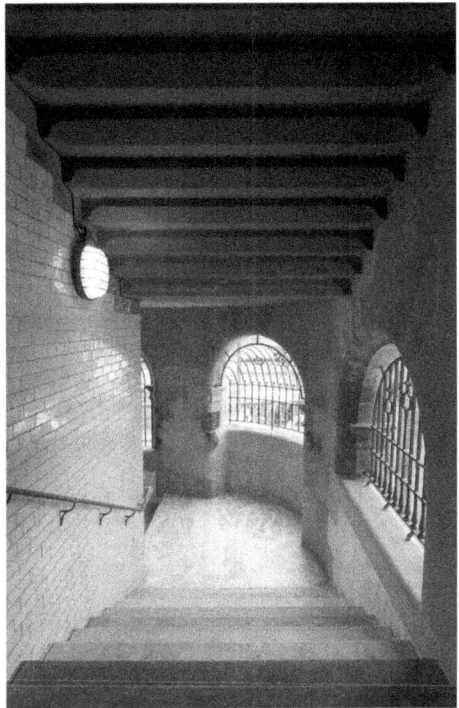

Figure 4.1 Martin Creed: The Scotsman Steps (Work No. 1059)

Notes

1 Tom Eccles and Martin Creed, 'Interview' Martin Creed, *Martin Creed: Works* (London: Thames and Hudson, 2010) pg. Xiv.
2 Although this might chime with Battcock's definition of Minimalism as *complex*, that is as an act of affirmation that sits within an established tradition of modern art and refers to its both its stylistic and conceptual genealogy, 'Minimal Art is not a negation of past art, or a nihilistic gesture. Indeed, it must be understood that by not doing something one can instead make a fully affirmative gesture, that the Minimal artist is engaged in an appraisal of the past and present, and that he frequently finds present aesthetic and sociological behaviour both hypocritical and empty. One could object that this attitude is merely a rationalization of an art form involved with nothing, but this is not the case. Minimal style is extremely complex. The artist has to create new notions of scale, space, containment, shape and object. He must reconstruct the relationship between art as object and between object and man.' Battcock, 'Introduction,' Gregory Battcock, *Minimal Art: A Critical Anthology* (London: Studio Vista, 1969) pg. 26. Emphasis added.

3 Every work is given an individual number, which is assigned when the work is first exhibited and is accompanied with a title. For example in the book *Martin Creed: Works*, the first piece presented is *Work No. 3, Yellow Painting* (1986), an abstract painting of yellow acrylic on canvas. See Martin Creed, *Martin Creed: Works* (London: Thames and Hudson, 2010).

4 https://www.bbc.co.uk/news/entertainment-arts-19001529

5 Barbara Rose, 'ABC Art,' in Gregory Battcock (ed.) *Minimal Art: A Critical Anthology* (London: Studio Vista, 1969) pg. 277.

6 Barbara Rose, 'ABC Art,' in Gregory Battcock (ed.) *Minimal Art: A Critical Anthology* (London: Studio Vista, 1969) pg. 281.

7 Carl Andre, 'Preface to Stripe Painting,' in Kristine Stiles & Peter Selz (eds.) *Theories and Documents of Contemporary Art: A Sourcebook of Artists' Writings* (Berkeley: University of California Press, 1996) pg. 147.

8 Quoted in Harold Rosenberg, *The De-Definition of Art* (Chicago, IL: University of Chicago Press, 1983) pg. 125.

9 Kristine Stiles and Peter Selz (eds.), 'Questions to Stella and Judd by Bruce Glaser,' in *Theories and Documents of Contemporary Art: A Sourcebook of Artists' Writings* (Berkeley: University of California Press, 1996) pp. 117–124.

10 Interview with Michael Craig Martin, 'The Oak Tree and the Lemon,' *Art Quarterly* (Autumn 2013) pg. 58.

11 Massimiliano Gioni, 'The System of Objects,' in Martin Creed (ed.) *Works* (London: Thames and Hudson, 2010) pg. xx.

12 For more on art history as a system, see Francis Halsall, 'Attractors and Locked-In Art: Art History as a Complex System,' in Sjoerd Van Tuinen (ed.) *Speculative Art Histories* (Edinburgh: Edinburgh University Press, 2017), pp. 39–60.

13 Arturo Schwarz, *The Complete Works of Marcel Duchamp* (New York: Harry N. Abrams, 1969) pp. 18–19.

14 In doing so, Warhol was repeating Duchamp's concept of the infrathin (inframince) in which the latter discussed in his posthumously published Notes, that is the imperceptible difference between things that can never be properly defined or discerned through aesthetic judgement including phenomena such as 'Magnifying glass for touching infrathin. The warmth of a seat (that had just been vacated) is infrathin.' Marcel Duchamp, in P. Matisse & P. Hulten (eds.) *Notes* (Paris: Centre national d'art et de culture Georges Pompidou/Flammarion, 1980/1999) pg. 21.

15 Arthur Danto, *The Transfiguration of the Commonplace* (Cambridge, MA: Harvard University Press, 1982), pg. 90.

16 Arthur Danto, *The Transfiguration of the Commonplace* (Cambridge, MA: Harvard University Press, 1982) pg. 94. Elsewhere Danto described this as:

> An object *o* is then an artwork only under an interpretation *I*, where *I* is a sort of function that transfigures *o into a work: I(o) = W*. Then even if *o* is a perceptual constant, variations in *I* constitute different works. Now *o* may be looked at, but the work has to be achieved, even if the achievement is immediate and without any conscious effort on the observers part.
>
> (pg. 125)

17 John Roberts, *Skill and Deskilling in Art after the Readymade* (London: Verso Books, 2007).

18 Clement Greenberg, 'Towards a Newer Laocoon,' *Partisan Review* 7 (1940) pp. 299–300.

19 Matthew Higgs, 'Martin Creed 20 Questions,' in Martin Creed (ed.) *Works* (London: Thames and Hudson, 2010) pg. xxx [original punctuation].

20 https://www.fruitmarket.co.uk/scotsman-steps/ [accessed, 1st December 2018].

References

Andre, Carl, 'Preface to Stripe Painting,' in Kristine Stiles & Peter Selz (eds.) *Theories and Documents of Contemporary Art: A Sourcebook of Artists' Writings* (p. 147), Berkeley: University of California Press, 1996

Battcock, Gregory, *Minimal Art: A Critical Anthology*, London: Studio Vista, 1969

Creed, Martin, *Martin Creed: Works*, London: Thames and Hudson, 2010

Creed, Martin, 'The Oak Tree and the Lemon (Interview with Michael Craig Martin)', *Art Quarterly* (Autumn 2013) pp. 56–63

Danto, Arthur, *The Transfiguration of the Commonplace*, Cambridge, MA: Harvard University Press, 1982

Duchamp, Marcel, 'Inframince' in P. Matisse & P. Hulten (eds.) *Notes* (pp. 21–36), Paris: Centre national d'art et de culture Georges Pompidou/Flammarion, 1980/1999

Gioni, Massimiliano, 'The System of Objects,' in Martin Creed (ed.) *Works* (pp. xx–xxiv), London: Thames and Hudson, 2010

Greenberg, Clement, 'Towards a Newer Laocoon', *Partisan Review*, 7 (1940) pp. 296–310

Halsall, Francis, 'Attractors and Locked-In Art: Art History as a Complex System', in Sjoerd Van Tuinen (ed.) *Speculative Art Histories* (pp. 39–60), Edinburgh: Edinburgh University Press, 2017

Higgs, Matthew, 'Martin Creed 20 Questions,' in Martin Creed (ed.) *Works* (pp. xxviii–xxiii), London: Thames and Hudson, 2010

Roberts, John, *Skill and Deskilling in Art after the Readymade*, London: Verso Books, 2007

Rose, Barbara, 'ABC Art,' in Gregory Battcock (ed.) *Minimal Art: A Critical Anthology* (pp. 274–298), London: Studio Vista, 1969

Rosenberg, Harold, *The De-Definition of Art*, Chicago, IL: University of Chicago Press, 1983

Schwarz, Arturo, *The Complete Works of Marcel Duchamp*, New York: Harry N. Abrams, 1969

Stiles, Kristine, and Selz, Peter (eds.) *Theories and Documents of Contemporary Art: A Sourcebook of Artists' Writings*, Berkeley: University of California Press, 1996

5   Theaster Gates and Systems of Improvisation and Entrepreneurship

Theaster Gates is an entrepreneur, improviser and trickster. He exemplifies the free agent or 'do-it-yourself'er' who uses systems and platforms to the advantage of themselves and others; and in doing so, there is enormous generosity in what he does. Gates operates as a cultural agent and an entrepreneur who, like Liam Gillick (albeit with different outcomes), mobilises a number of different platforms as mediums for his practice including art institutions, real estate and archives, and consequently explores and exploits instances of *dispersion* across social systems. Hence, relations within systems that are amongst other things, legal, economic, cultural and architectural, are opened up to observation, experience and scrutiny.

He is perhaps best known for his project, *Dorchester Projects*. This began in 2009. Since then, the artist has acquired and renovated several abandoned properties in Chicago's South Side, an area that is historically associated with social deprivation, neglect and a predominantly Black population. These have been turned into cultural spaces including studios, performance spaces, libraries and archives that connect with communities both local and further afield. In doing so, Gates was working with a number of different social systems including real estate and property, grant applications, the existing communities of people who live in the areas, and the subsequent emergent relations between people, objects and environments.

Gates's practice involves a direct engagement with materiality such as clay, tar or architecture. Hence, there is always an aesthetic dimension to his work; it is never intended to be solely conceptual. However, rather than understanding the stuff he works with as the primary object of his practice, his work does not merely involve the creation of objects, but rather the use of objects to interrogate dispersed relations within social systems. Gates's objects point to the material excess of social systems, and the objects he works with are indices of those systems. Those objects can be positioned across different platforms (such as museums) and in doing so represent elements of those systems in different contexts.

Gates's background involved the study of town planning and ceramics in America, religious studies in South Africa and pottery in Japan; he was also a

DOI: 10.4324/9781003315322-6

singer in a gospel choir and spoken-word artist. The horizons for his practice are, therefore, not institutional fine art but rather collaborative practices of planning, craft and entrepreneurship. However, as I argue here, his practice as a collaborator and entrepreneur is not driven merely by business interests. Instead, Gates uses strategies of entrepreneurship, improvisation and mischief to play with multiple identities and explore forms of collectivity, creativity and conviviality.

The Materiality of Dispersion

Gates has said that he's 'not interested in making beautiful objects.'[1] If Gates is taken at his word, then the objects he makes might be best interpreted not as beautifully constructed entities, or even signifiers in a symbolic system. Instead, they can be understood as material indices of complex relations in social systems and in particular Black and African American histories. Materiality is a key element of the subject matter of all of Gates's work, and through this concern with materiality, his work becomes a means of invoking, interrupting and commenting on dispersed social systems.

Take, for example, a series of black paintings that he produced using tar, *Painting Black With Kettle,* (2012). One way of reading these is to relate them to art movements such as Arte Povera, and their concern with everyday materials; or to experiments in abstraction sitting in an art historical lineage reaching from Constructivism to the monochromes of Ad Reinhardt. However, this would efface the material index being evoked. The tar paintings are made out of tar which refers specifically to Gates's biography. His father was a roofer who, when he retired, gave Gates the tar kettle that he used.[2] Alongside Gates's own family history, there is an allusion here to manual labour in general, via roofing, which sets the objects into a different set of concerns and question to those of Formalist Modernist Abstraction, relating, instead, to manual practices, craft and so forth.

Civil Tapestries, *Flag Series* (2012) is part of an ongoing series of works of collages made from fire hoses. These can also be placed alongside similar examples in the Duchampian use of appropriated objects put on the walls such as in the work of Robert Rauschenberg or Jasper Johns where there is a clear visual similarity in the use of lettering on the hoses. But what also going on here are references to complex histories of which the objects are indices. Specifically, the fire hoses evoke those that were used to control crowds during civil rights marches in America, particularly around 1968.

A concern with materiality is also manifest in work such as the sculpture *Black Madonna* (2018), a figure modelled in bronze and tar after a replica of a medieval depiction of Mary, the mother of Christ, with a child. It was exhibited as part of an exhibition of the same name at the Kunstmuseum Basel (2018). The sculpture takes the sculptural image of the mother of Christ as a *sedes sapientiae* (throne of wisdom) from its religious context and repurposes and repositions it within a gallery space. The fact that it is Black evokes complex race relations in relation to institutional histories and organised religion. Further, Gates has juxtaposed that with the sign reading 'Hardware,' suggesting that this is merely a type of everyday object or even a simple commodity for sale at a local shop. The word 'Hardware' calls attention to the materiality of the object.

Rebuild Foundation

The *Rebuild Foundation* incorporates a number of initiatives located in Chicago's South Side, a historically low-income area of social exclusion, with a largely Black community. Its stated mission is to demonstrate: 'the impact of innovative, ambitious and entrepreneurial cultural initiatives, and is enriched by three core values. Black people matter, Black spaces matter, and Black objects matter.'

It began in 2009 with *Dorchester Projects*, an abandoned two-story property, which Gates renovated into a library, slide archive and food kitchen. Dorchester Projects was originally intended as a two-year project, but has since developed into a larger project that identifies as an artist-led, community-based platform for art, cultural development and neighbourhood transformation that 'supports artists and strengthens communities by providing free arts programming and creating new cultural amenities on the South Side of Chicago.' Ongoing community development under the aegis of *Dorchester Art + Housing Collaborative* (DA + HC) includes the $10 million project on the renovation of a derelict housing block on Dante-Harper Avenues, where working with local architect Landon Bone Baker affordable housing for artists and cultural workers was created.

Besides architecture, there is also the 'manufacturing platform' *Dorchester Industries*, established to both create furniture and interior design 'using exceptional but often overlooked materials sourced throughout the City of Chicago' and train people in building, craft and design skills. Dorchester Industries is managed as a brand and company with profits used to 'promote culture-based, artist-led, neighborhood-driven community revitalization.'

At the heart of all of Gates's projects with the *Rebuild Foundation*, both geographically and conceptually, is the *Stony Island Arts Bank*. This is a handsome neo-classical building built in 1923 (by William Gibbons Uffendell) as *Stony Island State Savings Bank*, a community-based savings and loan bank. By the 1980s, the building was derelict and was eventually sold to Theaster Gates by the City of Chicago for $1 in the understanding that he would raise funds in order to renovate the centre and turn it specifically into an arts venue. Today, it is claimed, the initiative provides the South Side of Chicago with: '17,000 square feet of space for innovation in contemporary art and archival practice' (Figure 5.1).

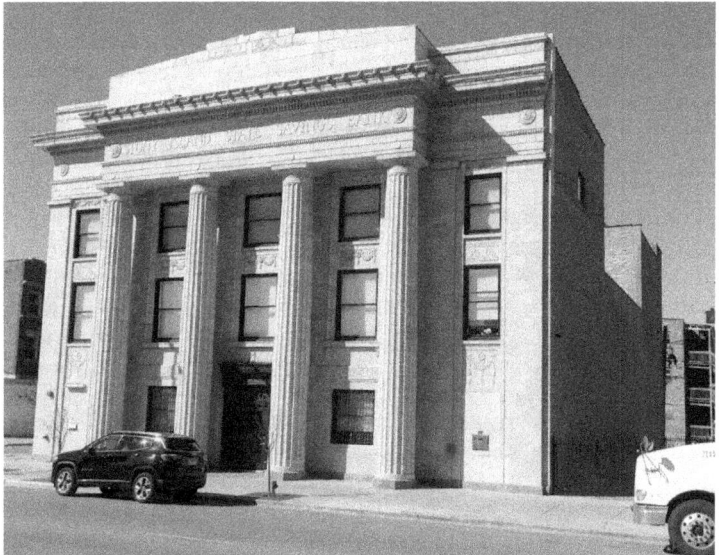

Figure 5.1 Stony Island Trust and Savings Bank Building

Stony Island Arts Bank also conceptually exemplifies Gate's project with the *Rebuild Foundation* that is literally a disused bank. As a financial institutional, this was once at the heart of the community and social system and has since been repurposed to have a different social function as a site of community engagement and interaction. Being a bank brings resonance to the project, because Gates is not only engaging in actual financial capital but also creating social and cultural capital.

The bank as a site of financial, social *and aesthetic* value is illustrated in the means by which the project came about through a process of what Gates calls profitable philanthropy. Gates took marble from the disused building and turned them into physical bonds each engraved with details as if they were enlarged stone versions of the familiar paper ones. In 2013, 100 of these stone bonds were made and sold at the art fair, Art Basel for $5,000 each, hence transforming artistic into fiscal capital in an act of creative entrepreneurship.

Currently, *Stony Island Arts Bank* includes a number of different archives which Gates has collected over the years and uses in education and artistic contexts. They are integral to the various different presentations that Gates makes of his work in galleries and other institutional settings. The archives are important records of Black culture that might otherwise have dissipated or disappeared. The archiving process began with the gift of a collection of over

60,000 glass lantern slides used for the teaching of art history at the University of Chicago. Here are objects that are doubly obsolete not only technologically, but also as tokens of a cannon of art history that has subsequently been challenged and expanded through processes of critique and decolonisation. Along with the slides is the archive of the Johnson Publishing Company, which is a collection of books and periodicals donated by the company that published the magazine, *Ebony* and *Jet*, which reflected on Black culture. These publications are complemented by the in-house library used by the workers, writers and editors of the company. There is also the collection of the DJ Frankie Knuckles personal vinyl records. Frankie Knuckles, often called the godfather of house music, was a key figure in the Chicago dance scene. He was one of the very first DJs to perfect the art of mixing one record into the other, and was also known for the way in which he would play disco tracks from vinyl overlaying drum beats, synthesised sounds, drum machines and so on over these. This has proved incredibly important and influential in the development of Black popular music and its reception by a diverse range of audiences. In addition, there is the troubling Edward J. Williams Collection. This is a collection of around 40,000 objects depicting Black people representing a collecting tradition known as negrobilia. Often, these are stereotypical images of Black people that are derogatory and deeply offensive. Williams began collecting these items over 30 years in part to remove them from public circulation but also as a kind of a historical archive for the way in which Black people were represented and understood in public spheres and popular imaginations.

Representation

Gates uses institutional platforms, such as museums and other spaces of exhibition, to represent various elements of the archives and his practice to the public such as in *Assembly Hall* his first major retrospective in Minneapolis (2019–2020). The Walker described this as a Gesamtkunstwerk in which the whole gallery was turned into a total work of art. It included material from the collections of slides, journals and 'Negrobilia' alongside ceramic pieces housed in four constructed environments evoking conditions of display from bourgeois living rooms to anthropological museums. Gates speaks of exhibition in terms of 'resurrections' referring to the rehabilitation of old objects in new spaces whilst also examining their historical and social contexts.

Arguably, the objects presented are drawn from material culture and, as such, are not presented as art. This is to say that Gates seems to be concerned with representing particular cultural histories via material culture and objects, rather than engaging in particular art histories. In other words, the positioning of these objects within a gallery space doesn't evoke any notions of a Duchampian, strategy of the Readymade, or repurposing of objects that are then turned into art by virtue of their institutional setting. Likewise, Gates doesn't seem to be engaged in a particular form of Institutional Critiques, such as we see in certain strategies within conceptual art like Han Haacke, for example, where there is a direct engagement with the fabric and the system of the museum to engage in a critique of that institutional space. Instead, Gates is mobilising objects in public spaces to demonstrate that those physical objects are indices of, and represent in material form, complex relations in social systems.

Another example of Gates using an exhibition platform as a means of representing one cultural context in a very different one is his participation in dOCUMENTA (13) (2012) in Kassel in Germany. In the *12 Ballads for the Huguenot House*, Gates collaborated with a number of groups. These included trainee workers from Chicago and Kassel who restored the historic building in Kassel using, in part, materials that had been taken from the restored Chicago buildings featured in the Rebuild Foundation projects and shipped to Kassel. Following the restoration (which was still ongoing as the public began to visit), the site was activated as a venue for invited performers and agents and a meeting place for social events. Regular Gates collaborators from Chicago, *The Black Monks of Mississippi*, gave improvised performances of blues, soul and gospel, effectively re-presenting element of the experiences and culture of Black people from Chicago in central Germany.

In both of the above examples, Gates uses the exhibition as a platform to represent an aspect of Chicago and in particular Gates's own social network within the context of the systems of contemporary art. As such, it is comparable to other representations of urban social systems in different contexts such as the 2022 Superbowl half-time show or the television show *The Wire*. At the Superbowl (held in SoFi Stadium in Inglewood, California), the hip hop culture of 90s Los Angeles was presented by performances from artists including: Eminem, 50 Cent, Dr Dre, Snoop Dogg, Mary J Blige (and others) in a stage set that recreated of elements of a local Compton neighbourhood in LA including the Martin Luther King Jnr monument that stands outside the City Hall; burger joint, *Tam's Burgers*; and a typical Compton house. Likewise, David Simon, the creator of *The Wire*, has been quite clear that the scope of the TV show extends beyond the specific context of Baltimore[3] to represent the social systems, such as law, education and media that, according to Niklas Luhmann, comprise a contemporary social system.

My argument is that Gates uses material objects as indices of social relations in order to represent those social relations across different exhibitionary platforms. Thus, as with the other examples in this book, (most notably, Creed) his practice sits in a different space to that traced by the dominant art historical trajectory away from modernism through conceptualism, Institutional Critique, Minimalism, etc. In conceptualism and the linguistic turn, there is a move to the dematerialisation of the art object, and the proposal that art has mutated into a form of philosophy. As, Kosuth says in *Art After*

Philosophy, works of art should be considered analytic rather than aesthetic propositions:

> viewed within their context – as art – they provide no information whatsoever about any matter of fact. A work of art is a tautology in that it is a presentation of the artist's intention, that is, he is saying that that particular work of art is art, which means, is a definition of art.[4]

In Gates, we see the opposite assumption that exhibited works are not analytic propositions, but actually material facts. And whether they are art or not might be beside the point.

Within the complex histories of race, particularly in North America, strategies of Institutional Critique are exemplified by Fred Wilson's incredibly influential work *Mining the Museum* from 1992. Wilson embedded himself in the Maryland Historical Society in Baltimore, and took objects from the collection and juxtaposed them side by side to reveal the hidden, complex and deeply troubling history of race relations embedded within social histories. These were highlighted through the juxtaposition of objects such as metalwork and valuable objects alongside slave manacles or a Ku Klux Klan costume and a cot. In a famous example, antique chairs from the 18th and 19th centuries are put in positions facing a whipping post that would have been used for the punishment of slaves. The reason that this is such an important and powerful show is that it engaged in a particular museum collection, and engages in a particular form of Institutional Critique couched in terms of race relations in America. It therefore can be read alongside other forms of Institutional Critique, including minimalism and conceptualism that were taking place within the art historical contexts of North America and Europe in the late 1960s and 1970s.

Gates, though, is doing something very different. He's not necessarily engaging in particular institutions, but is rather using various institutions as platforms to present material objects as the indices and means of representing the various different social relations that his work is all about. As he says: 'I want artists to understand that in the absence of a gallery or a museum, they have the capacity to invent the platform by which they can express their beliefs.'[5]

Entrepreneur of Relations

Considering Gates's uses of platforms including *Dorchester Projects* and *Dorchester Industries*, he is, in some respects, the main product of his practice. He is also, in Foucault's words, an entrepreneur of himself, and this often forms part of the critique of Gates. Rick Perlstein, for example, has compared Gates with P.T. Barnum, the famous 19th-century showman and a

'Real-Estate Artist'[6] proposing that his primary mediums are himself and his buildings. A similar critique is levelled by Gogarty:

> put cynically, Gates' ecological system involves the Rebuild Foundation acting as a feel-good money-laundering facility for the commercial art world and corporate developers, and this is what enables his status as a popularizer.[7]

Here, Gogarty is repeating Walter Benjamin's argument with regard to the problematic conflation of the commercial and creative spheres: 'bourgeois apparatus of production and publication is capable of assimilating, indeed of propagating, an astonishing amount of revolutionary themes without ever seriously putting into question its own continued existence or that of the class which owns it.'[8]

In other words, the conditions that Benjamin identifies also relate not only to Gates but also to the conditions of contemporary art in general as a product of neo-liberal capitalism and creative entrepreneurship. Certainly, many of the ways in which Gates talks about himself chime with this criticism. He writes:

> it's hard for me to get past value. I have a clear sense of what it means to be somebody, and that allows me to negotiate varying forms of capital. My body is capital, my brain is capital, my hands are capital, and the by-products of my hands are capital.[9]

As has been frequently observed, Gates also has a certain charismatic identity and has even referred to himself as autocratic, messianic and charismatic,[10] which facilitates his practice of cultural entrepreneurship. His practice involves capitalising on himself, as much as anything else. As Griffin writes on meeting him:

> Gates has a way of speaking that can make you feel like you're in the presence of someone with a gift for making dreams become reality. It is a quality shared by community leaders the world over, something often undersold as charisma, as if it were some kind of confidence trick. Encountered in its purest form, however, it is so much more than that: it is the ability not only to convince others of the potential for change, but to leverage that shared conviction to actually bring about that change.[11]

With statements such as this, he seems comparable to other entrepreneurs who mobilise aesthetic strategies for political ends and in doing so render their identity as a hyperbolic, perhaps fictional creation. The most extreme example of this is Donald Trump who writes in the *Art of the Deal* of what he and co-writer Tony Schwarz called 'truthful hyperbole':

> I play to people's fantasies. People may not always think big themselves, but they can still get very excited by those who do. That's why a little

hyperbole never hurts. People want to believe that something is the biggest and the greatest and the most spectacular.[12]

Although Gates might be seen to be doing something similar, he's actually performing in a very different way, in a very different spirit and with very different outcomes. Although he is unequivocal about the interconnection of his practice with business, he also acknowledges that he undertakes these activities through the rehearsal of multiple identities, thereby calling their fixed authenticity into question whilst acknowledging their contingency on the system of relations they sit within:

> So I am fifteen corporations. I am the chairman of a 501(c)3, the legal framework that allows an individual to be more than an individual while being an individual. The private foundation allows you to hide behind the opportunity of a tax shelter while being generous but without ever having to put yourself on the front line. A corporation allows me to buy one house with one corporation, and another house with another corporation, and so on, and so I become fifteen Theasters plus Theaster Gates Studio. Maybe what I am is really just an expanded individual, a complicated individual that both wants for himself and wants for the world. I'm not actually a utopic individual even though there are moments of utopic enterprise. I just don't want to be alone on Dorchester.[13]

Here, Gates articulates the two dimensions of what's at stake in terms of dispersed subjectivity. Through being a chairman of a number of different economic organisations, he operates as an entrepreneur of himself, capitalising upon his own identity. But in doing so, much like Gillick had said of himself, now he begins to disappear, perhaps, as an individual, and becomes absorbed within various different economic, social and cultural systems. And in doing so, he both rehearses and exemplifies conditions of the *Age of Dispersion*. He acknowledges the contingency of his identities by recognising their construction. On the fictional nature of his persona, he observes:

> I'm not performing 'real' architecture; in fact, I may not be performing 'real' art. I may not be a "real" artist. I may be a 'pseudo-artist,' by some standard of the real that has, connected to it, hierarchies of systematic accountability. I'm being coded.[14]

And in doing so articulates the difference between himself and a dangerous, autocratic narcissist like Trump.

In Chapter 2, I proposed an alternative reading of relational practices to those which see it as it as either participating in the spectacle and entertainment of late capitalism or offering some compensatory forms of community as a response. Conversely, I am interested here in those strategies that mimic some of the effects of dispersion of late capitalism but not to celebrate or submit to them but rather suggest a critique if not a bulwark against those effects.

Gates's form of creative entrepreneurship does this through the nurturing of alternative modes of sociality to those created by capitalism such as consumer groups or brand loyalty and is based, instead, on conviviality, generosity and shared values, shared cultures, shared crafts and shared histories. In doing so, Gates occupies spaces adjacent to those of institutionalised fine art and thus draws upon other traditions to offer alternative modes of sociality based on alternative practices, in particular, improvisation, community, community practices, ceramics and so on. In other words, his work is underwritten by a different model of creative practice to that of institutional fine art and in particular the lineage of practices after modernism including conceptualism and Institutional Critique.

Trickster: Fiction and Improvisation

If Gates's conviviality is understood as performative and coupled with a fluidity of identity, then two elements of his practice are emphasised: fiction and improvisation. Both of these are suggestive of a politics responsive to the *Age of Dispersion*.

For example, in his first public show *Plate Convergences* (2007) Gates staged a tribute to his mentor Shoji Yamaguchi at the exhibition.[15]At a dinner party, 100 diners were served up typical Southern food and Japanese food on ceramic plates made especially by Gates using materials and techniques particular to Mississippi. To give proceedings some historical heft, on the wall there are timeline-plotted relevant historical points including moments from the Ming Dynasty and slavery, and the birthdays of Yamaguchi and Gates.

Gates then entertained the guests, including Yamaguchi's son, with the remarkable story of Yamaguchi, a talented potter from Hiroshima who immigrated to Mississippi after World War 2. He had been drawn there by it being the source of a particular type of clay. There, he met and married a local African American woman and became involved in civil rights activism. They established pottery that also became a salon where people gathered to socialise, eat and discuss political issues. They also devised a unique ceramic style that both combined African American and Asian craft techniques and was particularly suited to African American cuisine. Yamaguchi met Gates in 1985 and mentored his developing ceramic practice. After the couple died in a car accident, their son developed their legacy through the Yamaguchi Institute.

Through this, and many similar events, Gates is fostering forms of conviviality that, in turn, nurture the creation of communities that exist, fleetingly, in particular times and spaces.

Crucially, Yamaguchi never existed and his son was played by an actor at the dinner. He is a fiction but a creative and useful one that is, at the very least, adjacent to the truth. Gates did visit Japan and study ceramic techniques there, and the complex histories of race relations in America are obviously very real. Gates brings people together to consider these complex relations in social systems through the performance of hospitality and the logic of the gift. This is not the form of gift as a form of a commodity, or the exchange of economic value, but the gift which is something ineffable. It is the creation of conviviality, and it's performed in the acts of generosity. Gates has talked about this form of generosity, such as creating the figure of Yamaguchi and inviting people into his world as a form of 'magic' by which he means the creation of something new.

Magic and potency and health in the community that I live in are important. They trump, in some cases, other forms of institutional generosity, or at least complement institutional generosity. A measured, politicized, charitable return is not the only form for being generous. More rudimentary forms of direct engagement and exchange have real and consequential value. New magic, in this sense, is the conditional apparatus that makes people want to share.[16]

In his use of fiction and magic, Gates is closer to the figure that Lewis Hyde calls the trickster rather than the businessman or entrepreneur. Hyde considers tricksters *lords of in-between* that are forever homeless and on the move. They are world makers or the creators of fictions, and, as such, are a model of the artist as an agent that disrupts the social order and creates new things. The trickster roves between spaces, disrupting things and engaging with various different forms of social interaction.

Another place where Gates embraces the unexpected is his ongoing collaboration with The Black Monks of Mississippi, a musical ensemble informed by the music of the Black American south including Gospel, Soul, folk and slave songs. Their identity is underpinned by collectivism, adherence to the form and tradition of the blues, which Gates believes is the most important strand in American music, and improvisation. On improvisation as a technique, writing about free jazz Andrian Kreye considers that surprising and miraculous moment when things all click into place and the musicians find 'The Pulse':

It is a collective climax of creativity and communication that can leap to the audience and create an electrifying experience. It's hard to describe, but it might be comparable to the moment when a surfer finds the point when the catalyst of the surfboard brings together the motor skills of his body and the forces of the swell of an ocean start in these few seconds of synergy on top of a wave. It is a fusion of musical elements though that defies common musical theory.[17]

Improvisation as a mode of collective decision-making and collective creation is not only a model of creative practice, but also a model of understanding the human. The improvising subject is not a mere individual, but a dispersed entity enmeshed within a number of creative and enabling relationships with other agents. Hence, in this model of the human as dispersed perhaps one also finds another model of politics, which is decentralised. An example of this can be seen in group activity such as Extinction Rebellion, and their non-hierarchical forms of decision-making. In the Extinction Rebellion Handbook, for example, they write:

> If we had to truly decentralize, the hierarchy must become a web. Instead of a top, there is a middle. The middle is breath, heart, and information. It empowers instead of commands. We flow organically together, like a flock of birds with no one leader, moved by our instincts of togetherness. We trust that we are all here for one shared purpose: system change.

This description of political organisation, in this case about protesting and mobilising against global climate change, understands it in the same way as an improvisatory aesthetic practice as well. That description could just as much describe a jazz quintet as much as it could describe the music produced by *The Black Monks of Mississippi*, which are also improvising together not fully knowing how things will turn out.

Conclusion

The origins Gates's practice as an entrepreneur, trickster and improviser do not lie in the studios and curricula of fine art. Instead, his work draws on different traditions including religious studies, ceramics, town planning and gospel. Therefore, much like some of the other artists in this book, his work doesn't concern itself with some of the main themes of Western modernism and post-modernism, including individual expression, Institutional Critique or forms of reflexive formalism. Clay, as both a substance and metaphor, lies at the heart of things.

Reflecting on his training as a ceramicist, Gates observed how working with clay provides unique ways of thinking about the world in terms of materiality, tactility and relations:

> Clay and its metaphor of transformation allowed me to imagine cities differently, that I as an artist had the capacity to change zoning policies, building code that hadn't been looked at in a hundred years, change the psyche of a city around what a neighborhood represented. In a place that had been crack-filled, and where people imagined that there was only violence, I was really excited to transport people's ideas about what happened in places.[18]

The malleability of clay and the particularities of ceramics provide a unique model of practice. It is one couched in terms of an interrogation of relations between creator and material where things are unpredictable and the maker is not fully in control of their medium. The potter doesn't know exactly how things will turn out; clay, like groups of people, can do unexpected things when fired.

Notes

1 Quoted in Carol Becker, Lisa Yun Lee and Achim Borchardt, *Theaster Gates* (London: Phaidon Press, 2015) pg. 44.

2 There might also be a reference here to the Tar-Baby, which could refer to the figure from African-American folklore and its use as an offensive term.

3 'The Wire was not about Jimmy McNulty. Or Avon Barksdale. Or Marlo Stanfield, or Tommy Carcetti or Gus Haynes. It was not about crime. Or punishment. Or the drug war. Or politics. Or race. Or education, labour relations or journalism. It was about the City. It is how we in the west live at the millennium, an urbanized species compacted together, sharing a common love, awe and fear of what we have rendered not only in Baltimore or St Louis or Chicago but in Manchester or Amsterdam or Mexico City as well.' David Simon, 'Introduction,' in Rafael Alvarez (ed.) *The Wire: Truth be Told* (New York: Pocket Books, 2010) pg. 10.

4 Joseph Kossuth, 'Art after Philosophy,' *Studio International* (October, 1969).

5 Gates, quoted in Carol Becker, Lisa Yun Lee and Achim Borchardt, *Theaster Gates* (London: Phaidon Press, 2015) pg. 20.

6 Rick Perlstein, 'There Goes the Neighborhood,' *The Baffler* (no. 28, July 2015).

7 Larne Abse Gogarty, 'Art and Gentrification,' *Art Monthly* 373 (February 2014) pg. 7.

8 Walter Benjamin, 'The Author as Producer' (trans. Heckman), *New Left Review*, 1/62 (July–August 1970), at: https://newleftreview.org/.

9 Tom McDonagh, 'Theaster Gates,' *Bomb*, #130 (Dec. 10th, 2004) at: https://bombmagazine.org/articles/theaster-gates/ (accessed, June 2022).

10 *"I don't think of myself as a good collaborator. I imagine myself as a kind of monopoly autocrat—messianic, charismatic—and so I want to suggest that there might be ways in which you can both believe in the possibility of the individual and believe in the possibility of the collective."* Theaster Gates, 'The Artist Corporation and the Collective,' *NKA: Journal of Contemporary African Art*, 34 (Spring 2014) pp. 74–79.

11 Jonathan Griffin, 'Brick by Brick,' *Apollo Magazine* (March, 2017) pp. 140–146.

12 Reynolds continues: *[Truthful Hyperbole] sounds like a contradiction in terms, but it cuts to the essence of how hype works: by making people believe in something that doesn't exist yet, it magically turns a lie into a reality. As the American saying goes, fake it 'til you make it. Bowie's manager Tony Defries used this technique to break the singer in America: travelling everywhere in a limo, surrounded by bodyguards he didn't need, Bowie looked like the star he wasn't yet, until the public and the media started to take the illusion for reality…. Early in his career, Trump grasped that – like a pop star – he was selling an image, a brand* Simon Reynolds, *Shock and Awe* (London: Faber, 2016).

13 Theaster Gates, 'The Artist Corporation and the Collective,' *NKA: Journal of Contemporary African Art*, 34 (Spring 2014) pp. 74–79.

14 Tom McDonagh, 'Theaster Gates,' *Bomb*, #130 (Dec. 10th, 2004) at: https://bombmagazine.org/articles/theaster-gates/ (accessed, June 2022).

15 Chicago's Hyde Park Art Center (HPAC).

16 Tom McDonough, 'Theaster Gates,' *Bomb*, #130 (Dec. 10th, 2004) at: https://bombmagazine.org/.
17 Andrian Kreye, 'Free Jazz,' *The Edge* (2011) at: https://www.edge.org/responsedetail/10599 (accessed, June 2022).
18 Quoted in Hesse McGraw, 'Theaster Gates: Radical Reform with Everyday Tools,' *Afterall*, 30 (Summer 2012) pp. 88–99.

References

Abse Gogarty, Larne, 'Art and Gentrification', *Art Monthly*, 373 (February, 2014) pp. 7–10

Alvarez, Rafael (ed.) *The Wire: Truth be Told*, New York: Pocket Books, 2010, p. 10

Becker, Carol, Lisa Yun Lee, and Achim Borchardt, *Theaster Gates*, London: Phaidon Press, 2015

Benjamin, Walter, 'The Author as Producer' (trans. John Heckman), *New Left Review*, 1/62 (July–August 1970), https://newleftreview.org/

Gates, Theaster, 'The Artist Corporation and the Collective', *NKA: Journal of Contemporary African Art*, 34 (Spring, 2014) pp. 74–79

Griffin, Jonathan, 'Brick by Brick', *Apollo Magazine* (March, 2017) pp. 140–146

Kossuth, Joseph, 'Art After Philosophy', *Studio International*, 178, no. 915 (October, 1969)

Kreye, Andrian, 'Free Jazz', *The Edge* (2011), https://www.edge.org/responsedetail/10599 (accessed, June 2022)

McDonagh, Tom, 'Theaster Gates', *Bomb*, #130 (Dec. 10th, 2004) https://bombmagazine.org/articles/theaster-gates/ (accessed, June 2022)

McGraw, Hesse, 'Theaster Gates: Radical Reform with Everyday Tools', *Afterall*, 30 (Summer 2012) pp. 88–99

Perlstein, Rick, 'There Goes the Neighborhood', *The Baffler*, no. 28 (July 2015), https://thebaffler.com/salvos/there-goes-the-neighborhood (accessed, 28 March 2023)

Reynolds, Simon, *Shock and Awe*, London: Faber, 2016

6 Hito Steyerl

In Defence of the Poor Manifest Image

Hito Steyerl works across multiple mediums and platforms including multi-media installations, films, extensive writing and lecturing. A central theme across all the practice is the interrogation of how multiple identities may be constructed and/ or effaced through the systems of media, entertainment and surveillance (which are very often the same systems). She proffers an engagement with these systems that is at once oblique, humorous and critical. In doing so, Steyerl's work explores the central claim of this book that understandings of the identity of both art and human subjectivity are congruent and that this congruence hinges on technology and systems of communication and control, in particular themes of spatial and temporal dislocation feature. She asks: 'What happened to time and space? Why are they broken and disjointed? Why is space shattered into container-like franchising modules, dark webs, civil wars, and tax havens replicating all over the world?'[1] Steyerl provides a model of dispersed subjectivity (and art) by providing a *manifest image* with it. But rather than this being a discrete or coherent entity, the manifest image in Steyerl's work is a *poor* one, that is one that is incoherent and dispersed across platforms, space and time. In other words, as she writes: 'contemporary art shows us the lack of a (global) time and space. Moreover, it projects a fictional unity onto a variety of different ideas of time and space, thus providing a common surface where there is none.'[2]

The identity of art has become dispersed across different mediums and platforms to serve as a spectacular form of lucrative entertainment. And, as has been repeated through the different discussions, this crisis of art has occurred simultaneous to moment that the horizon of human finitude, through ecological extinction or technological obsolescence, heaves into view. Steyerl interrogates some of these conditions of remediation and dispersion. Their practice explores the congruent crises of both the image and identity in the Age of Dispersion not to valorise these conditions, but to highlight some of their complexities (Figure 6.1).

All art exhibitions should be like this!

Over the summer months of 2022, the Royal Dublin Showgrounds (RDS) hosted the Irish premier of *Van Gogh Dublin*, an 'Immersive Art Attraction'

DOI: 10.4324/9781003315322-7

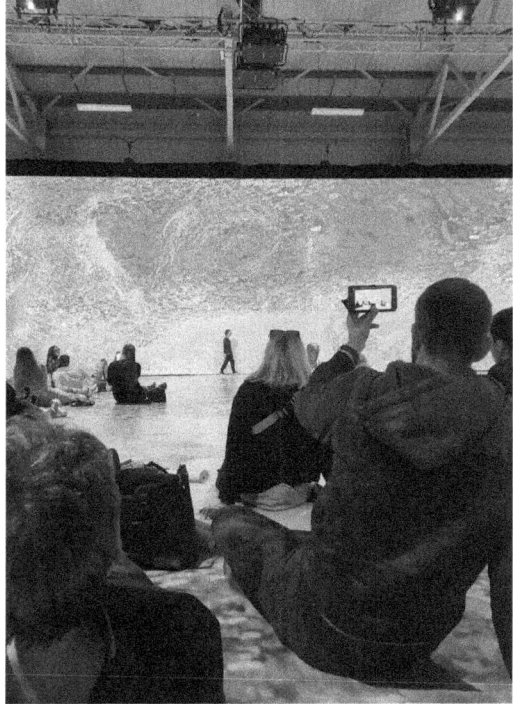

Figure 6.1 Van Gogh Dublin RDS – An Immersive Journey

featuring using AI technology to present copies of over 2,000 works of art 'in the style of the Gogh himself [in a] full 360 immersive landscape.' The event promised to allow:

> the viewer to become one with the art themselves... [and] Be enveloped in a world that is rendered using interdisciplinary experiences that fuse the beauty of art, design and technology with Dutch born post-impressionist painter Vincent Van Gogh.[3]

Viewers, it claimed, would not only be enveloped 'in the very brushstrokes of Van Gogh himself' to 'become part of a living breathing canvas' but also brought through 'the mind of the artist himself to experience the intensity, chaos and disorientation at the helm.' Having experienced this, the audience would then be prompted into: 'Calling into question the concept of everything [that is]: how science, philosophy and metaphysics converge to question all and suggest new possibilities.'

Across town, a very similar, or perhaps totally different, experience was offered. *The Van Gogh Exhibit in Dublin: The Immersive Experience* inviting people to:

> 'step into a 20,000 sq. ft. light and sound spectacular exhibit featuring two story projections of the artists' most compelling works.' Have you, the website asked, 'ever dreamt of stepping into a painting? Now you can with this exhibition that has been touring since 2017 with +5,000,000 visitors!'⁴

One review that the organisers posted on the site by Bev M. read 'Amazing! All art exhibitions should be like this! the immersive experience at the end was fantastic!' (sic).

These spectacular shows foreground some central themes of this book in relation to the concept of remediation. It's my argument here that if an understanding of art will always be underwritten by an understanding of what the human subject is, then there will be comparable instances of remediation in human experience. In other words, just as the paintings of Van Gogh can be turned into businesses offering immersive spectacular experiences, remediation is also a way of considering the human subject as something, which is being repurposed, repositioned and dispersed through various platforms.

Poor Images

The theme of the human subject being dispersed through platforms is a consistent theme of Steyerl's work. Here, I demonstrate this through considering three paradigmatic artworks: *How to Not Be Seen: A Fucking Didactic Educational.MOV File* (2013); *Liquidity Inc.* (2014); and *Factory of the Sun* (2015). Each of these uses the aesthetic of material distributed online such as GIFs, Memes, TikToks, Tumblr, fan tributes and home-made videos. The overall tone is one of black humour. These works are partly serious, partly absurd. The main themes are surveillance, embodiment, subjectivity and technology, and each has the central, repeating, subject of dispersed and diffuse images that are analogues for more general conditions of dispersion in experience.

How to Not Be Seen: A Fucking Didactic Educational.MOV File (2013) is a 14-minute HD video that also mimics an information film, providing a number of satirical lessons, given by an automated-sounding voice, for how to be 'unseen' in a time of 'total over-visibility.' The artist presents five ways to make oneself invisible: *1. Make something invisible for a camera; 2. Be invisible in plain sight; 3. Become invisible by becoming a picture; 4. Be invisible by disappearing;* and *5. Become invisible by merging into a world made of picture.*

The title is taken from a sketch from a Monty Python's Flying Circus sketch *How Not to Be Seen* (1970), which is a parody of an instructional film in which people attempt and fail to camouflage themselves and are blown up. The footage presented involves a hybrid of real and simulated imagery such as a virtual replica of an idealised community along with anonymous dancing figures in all-over body suits with no faces and repurposed film such as a video of the soul band The Three Degrees singing 'When Will I see you Again?' The film is anchored by two main, recurring, subjects: a site in the California desert of decommissioned US Air Force aerial-photography calibration targets; and the artist themselves as a protagonist. A central leitmotif of the piece is the iconography of targets, a sequence of lines and numbers in a square, which appear in the landscape, reproduced on different surfaces and painted onto Steyerl's face.

It offers strategies including camouflage and hacking alongside more sardonic takes on how people are rendered invisible or obsolete such as: 'being female and over fifty... being a disappeared person as an enemy of the state ...being a Wi-Fi signal moving through human bodies... being spam caught by a filter.' A central theme is how invisibility is a symptom of dispersion in global systems.

Liquidity Inc. (2014) combines a 30-minute HD video displayed on a large screen within an architectural installation comprising a blue seating structure cushioned with judo mats supported by scaffolding and blue panels on the walls and blue lighting that create a unified environment. The supporting structure feels provisional recalling, perhaps, makeshift infrastructure for emergency situations such as accommodation for refugees. Steyerl has said that the structure might also invoke a raft, which has the obvious connotation of migration. The film is framed as a documentary about Jacob Wood, former financial analyst for Lehman Brothers who lost his job in the economic crash of 2008 when the company, notoriously, went bankrupt. He subsequently became a mixed martial artist. It combines a similar mix of real and simulated material. Intercut with the story of Wood are simulated meteorological systems including floods and hurricanes and weather reports given by what appear to be guerrilla meteorologists in balaclavas hiding their faces. The reports they give claim that the weather phenomena are directly linked to the audiences' emotional states and underlying economic conditions. The central leitmotif of the piece is liquidity referring simultaneously to water, finance, data and even the contingent and fluctuating conditions of subjectivity in late capitalism. Weather is just one of the global systems that enmesh humans and yet are not 'steerable' by them.

Factory of the Sun (2015) was first shown in the German Pavilion at the Venice Biennale, 2015. It features a looped, 21-minute HD video played on a large screen and an accompanying immersive environment filled with collapsible beach chairs. The room is bathed in electric blue light and features a grid of florescent lights that most obviously recall the early 1980s sci-fi aesthetics of films such as *Tron* (1982). The film is more obviously fictional than *How Not to be Seen* and *Liquidity Inc.* in so far as there is a twin narrative and a central character Yulia, a video game maker. She tells her family story of immigration to Canada from the former Soviet Union where they had suffered persecution. Since moving, her brother has become famous for dancing online. His many fans have created animated versions of the dance. In a parallel narrative, there are workers who are similarly dancing but are doing so against their will in a motion-capture studio (Figure 6.2).

In both dances, the movement seems to be a source of power and energy and can be converted into light that can be manipulated. The dancers do so as an act of collective joy and perhaps in protest of authoritarian power and globalisation. In the factory, however, dancing is the labour that the dancers are alienated from. Here, the leitmotif is the light that emerges from the sun, digital screens and the actions of the dancers who are both workers, earning through their activities, and gamers playing, via avatars, on the platform, to secure tokens. Steyerl is gesturing to the fact that visible light is just a part of the spectrum of electromagnetic radiation, which is also the medium of various forms of communication that encircle the global system from radio waves to the pulses through fibre-optic cables. In doing so, the complex relationships between subjectivity, agency, economics and power in dispersed systems are highlighted.

Combined with the artistic (and pedagogical) practice, Steyerl also interrogates conditions of dispersion through her extensive and accomplished writings. In the essay 'Duty Free Art,' she considers one of the conditions of art through the phenomenon of Freeport art storage, that is art that is housed in tax-free zones that are independent of national sovereignty. For example, Shannon Free Zone, Ireland, was established beside an airport in 1959 as the first modern

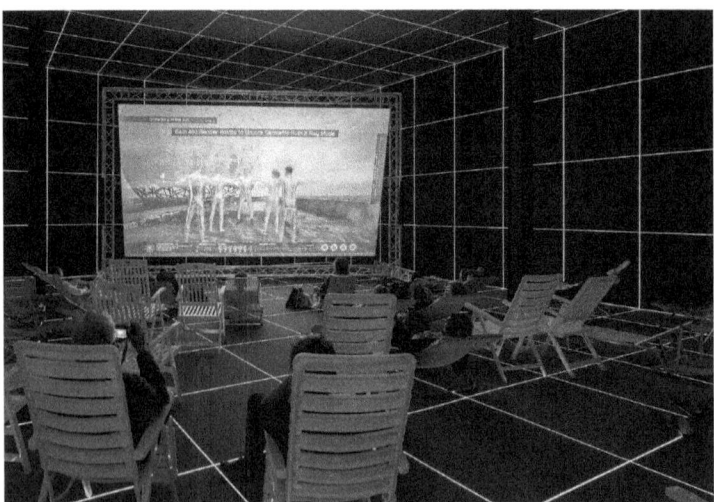

Figure 6.2 Hito Steyerl: Factory of the Sun (2015)

Freeport allowing for the transfer and storage of goods autonomous from state taxes and laws. Keller Easterling writes that these spaces are paradigmatic of the contemporary conditions of systems of global infrastructure. Such systems, Easterling argues, are 'new forms of polity' that are ungovernable because they fall outside of national jurisdiction. This infrastructure is, instead, subject to the unsteerable logic of *Extrastatecraft.* The freezone, the write, is:

> a highly contagious and globalized urban form and a vivid vessel of what I have termed extrastatecraft. A portmanteau meaning both outside of and in addition to statecraft, extrastatecraft acknowledges that multiple forces — state, non-state, military, market, non-market — have now attained the considerable power and administrative authority necessary to undertake the building of infrastructure.[5]

The art housed in such spaces occupies a very different space to that of the public museum as it was formulated by Habermas as an articulation of the post-enlightenment bourgeois sphere. In that earlier model, the museum, like the coffee house, theatre and salon, was a space in which judgements could be articulated, tested and debated and norms negotiated alongside emerging forms of social communication such as a free press. In contrast, the art housed in Freeports is not only available to public audiences, but also sits outside of any accessible public sphere. What if, Steyerl asks, the Freeport is 'one of the most important spaces in the world right now?'[6] If this is the case, it is because the Freeport and its contents exemplify the conditions of what Augé calls non-places,[7] such as airports or autobahns where specific identities and differences are effaced and flattened in spaces of commerce and transportation. Just as people in these places are in transit so too are objects. Hence, Steyerl argues, 'Contemporary art thus becomes a proxy for the global commons, for the lack of any common ground, temporality or space. It is defined by a proliferation of locations, and a lack of accountability.'[8]

In another essay, Steyerl discusses how these conditions are given form and made visible in the figure of the 'poor image.' These are images in flux of bad quality or poor resolution characteristic of images copied, distributed, ripped, remixed and experienced across different networks, platforms and screens. They are images of events hastily documented on phones or tablets, or gifs and memes circulated on messaging apps. They are, Steyerl says, errant and itinerant, and they are ghosts, previews and thumbnails. The significance of poor images lies in how they articulate and represent more general underlying conditions of collective experience, not through metaphor but rather as a literal embodiment of the same effects of dispersion experienced by us all. Steyerl writes:

> poor images present a snapshot of the affective condition of the crowd, its neurosis, paranoia, and fear, as well as its craving for intensity, fun, and distraction. The condition of the images speaks not only of countless

transfers and reformattings, but also of the countless people who cared enough about them to convert them over and over again, to add subtitles, reedit, or upload them.[9]

Remediation

A repeated theme in all of the works so far introduced is a consideration of the effects of presenting the conditions and effects of one medium through another. This process of remediation[10] is ubiquitous in contemporary experience from contemporary television broadcasts including content from other platforms such as Twitter or the seemingly infinite amount of uploaded, remixed and repurposed content on YouTube. Remediation as it is coined and unpacked by Bolter and Gruisin is a reconsideration of ideas previously explored by Marshall McLuhan when he argued that the content of one medium is always another one. Although they were writing about (so-called) New Media Art at the end of the 1990s, the definition still stands as the description of repurposing one medium through another. As a result of remediation, certain qualities of a medium will be emphasised by virtue of the way in which they are represented or 'refashioned' in another medium. A painting, for example, when photographed becomes a flattened image alongside others, yet when filmed different relations between formal elements might be emphasised. The same thing happens with architecture; a photograph of a three-dimensional building tends to reduce the three-dimensional space to a set of formal relations in two dimensions. Bolter and Gruisin were particularly interested in how the then new media such as video and online presentation was a continuation of a historical process of remediation such as photography remediating painting followed by film remediating theatre and photography and then television remediating film, theatre, radio and so on.

In parallel to art changing according to these processes of remediation, the experiences of the human subject are also transforming. This resonates with what Nicolas Bourriaud called *Post Production,* also back in the late nineties, to refer to the way in which the role of the artist has changed, and that artists are now rather like DJs or computer programmers, that is remixing or reprogramming pre-existing material rather than generating new material. To consider this in the field of text, for example, Kenneth Goldsmith writing in *Uncreative Writing*[11] speaks about a new legibility that comes about when we are online, when text becomes remediated through online platforms, when it's read on the screen rather than off the page. Writing on this new illegibility of text, he claimed that when online:

> Our reading habits seem to be imitating the way machines work: we could even say that online, by an inordinate amount of skimming in order to comprehend all the information passing before our eyes, we parse text- a binary process of sorting language-more than we read it. So this work demands a thinkership, not a readership.[12]

Claire Bishop also addressed the theme of remediation through 'repurposing' in the digital era leading, perhaps, finally to the often predicted obsolescence of art:

> Faced with the infinite resources of the Internet, selection has emerged as a key operation: We build new files from existing components, rather than creating from scratch. [...]Questions of originality and authorship are no longer the point; instead, the emphasis is on a meaningful recontextualiza-tion of existing artifacts. [...] If the digital means anything for visual art, it is the need to take stock of this orientation and to question art's most treasured assumptions.[13]

There are parallels between these forms of remediation facilitated by digital technologies in what they mean for art and also what they might mean for how we understand human subjectivities. It has now become commonplace, for example, to recognise that our own identities are being remediated through various different platforms of social media and that those various different platforms facilitate different personalities that are sort of being played out in different spheres and different platforms. I might have one identity as an antagonist, for example, on Twitter, whereas I might be a sports person on Strava, a dater on Tinder or an academic on academia.edu.

Twitter and Strava alongside other platforms create a way in which per-sonal identity may also be remediated. A consequence of this is the gamifi-cation of relationships such as presented by Steyerl in *Factory of the Sun*. Social media also follows the logic of gaming in which an avatar is created (disappointed, middle-aged white man, for example) and played for rewards. In older games such as Pac-Man, gamers collected coins and avoided ghosts, whilst in the age of Twitter or Instagram, it is 'likes' that are collected and being ghosted or cancelled that's to be avoided.

As humans become more integrated into this technology, their senses of iden-tity begin to become dispersed or degraded. As Elon Musk frequently observes humans are already a cyborg, or non-human, post-human or a trans-human, Musk is claiming that because we are so well integrated with our phones and our computers we are already being remediated by that technology. Wearable technology, such as smartwatches or rings, measures all sorts of different biom-etric data, including heart rate, blood pressure, variable heart rate and sleeping time. If this remediation is taking place via the body, then that body, as the site of subjectivity, becomes remediated through various different platforms and as a result becomes dependent on those platforms to be legible.

The implication of the body in these processes of remediation introduces the possibility of its effects on erotic experience. Consider, for example, how users of an interface and service like *OnlyFans* are facilitated as creators of explicit sexual content by directly managing the relationships with their sub-scribers. In doing so, they become responsible not only for their own con-tent but also for their earning. In considering the effect of the availability of online pornography, in the *Butterfly Effect*, John Ronson points out that 'erectile dysfunction is up 1000% in 16 to 21 year olds since 2007. But what happened in 2007? Free streaming porn.' Ronson is here echoing something that had been observed by Irvine Welsh previously, when he made the slightly throwaway but still meaningful comment:

> That's the thing with sex work, it always comes down to the most basic of formulas. If you really want to see how capitalism operates, never mind Adam Smith's pin factory, this is the place to study.[14]

alluding to the reference to Adam Smith in the *Communist Manifesto*. Pornography is the site where the cutting edges of capitalism and technology meet.

Manifest Images

To return to one of this book's key arguments, there is equivalence in metaphors of human self-understanding and dominant technologies. George Zarkadakis identifies six main metaphors for human consciousness each related to a different technology: clay infused with spirit; fluids and humours; mechanical processes; electricity and life-force; telegraphy and internal communication; and the computer. Each of these metaphors places humans in the horizon of particular worlds with both potentials and limits.[15] The computer metaphor, for example, is a useful means of understanding cognitive processes in terms of information processing and the shuttling of ions along axons as signals within a cognising system of communication and control. However, this is limiting in being based on the von Neumann architecture that is present in nearly all computers. This metaphor of the mind as computer requires a dualism, that of software and hardware, that duplicates the Cartesian dichotomy of ideas (mind) and things (body) and thus has coded into it the attendant philosophical problems such as how they might interact.

The normative, commonplace (or folk psychological) ways in which humans understand themselves were tered the *manifest image* by the philosopher Wilfrid Sellars. In distinction to the *manifest image* was what he called the *scientific image*, that is the conception of reality that is observed and underwritten by current scientific understandings. The manifest image describes the world as it is perceived and experienced in everyday life. The scientific image, however, describes the world as it is observed by scientific methods and apparatus, which detect entities and behaviour beyond the limits of unaided perception. For example, we experience an object such as a table through a combination of perceptual informed and culturally framed experiences and expectations and not as a complex combination of particles and forces that can be parsed according to Newtonian or Quantum physics.

For Sellars even though the manifest and scientific images use different mechanisms and vocabularies to describe the world, they also inform one another. This explains how the metaphors of self-understanding adapt and develop over time. For example, since Copernicus' observations are now generally accepted it is understood that the earth travels round the sun (and not vice-versa) even though only a very small number of humans (astronauts, scientists) have experienced the evidence for this first hand. On the one hand, the manifest image provides a normative and intersubjective framework for understanding ourselves in relation to each other:

'in which we think of one another as sharing the community intentions which provides the ambience of principles and standards (above all those which make meaningful discourse and rationality itself possible) within which we live our own individual lives.[16]

On the other hand, the scientific image gestures towards an objective, non-human world autonomous from norms and cultural influence. Sellars proposed that even though the two images were in dialogue, they were fundamentally incompatible and that ultimately the scientific image, which was objective and thus descriptively superior, would completely replace the redundant manifest image.

However, already at the turn of the 20th century, the originator of Phenomenology, Edmund Husserl, recognised the tensions between what Sellars was to call the manifest and scientific images. In a puzzling little paper, which remained, tellingly, unpublished in his lifetime, he offered a phenomenological account of the motionless-ness of the Earth. The Earth, he claimed, does not move, at least not in relation to us. Rather, we move in relation to it. He wrote:

Movement occurs on or in the earth, away from it or off it. In the primordial shape of its representation, the earth itself does not move and does not rest; only in relation to it are movement and rest given as having their sense of movement and rest.[17]

His insight was that scientific knowledge doesn't and can't ever fully describe the world as it is experienced. That is, the understanding of an objective world, one observed by scientific description, is not something merely, passively, given to consciousness but rather something actively *achieved* by it. Husserl shows us that, whilst conscious, one can never escape experience. It is not possible to escape, despite Sellars' wishes, the manifest image.

Recognising the impossibility of this flight from experience recently, the physicist Sean Carroll (echoing the philosophical arguments of Van Fraassen) argued that the Manifest and Scientific images, instead of being mutually exclusive, can be reconciled. This means accepting that there can be different, sometimes competing, conceptions that humans have of themselves. This, Carroll calls *Poetic Naturalism*, which is a position that accepts: 'the usefulness of each way of talking in its appropriate circumstances, and works to show how they can be reconciled with one another.'[18] However, my argument is rather than giving a reconciliation, Steyerl gives us a different type of manifest image, one that is degraded. This image is informed by prevalent technological conditions in which information and identities are dispersed throughout platforms and systems of communication and control. It is an image in breakdown.

Conclusion

Steyerl presents the contemporary effects of remediation as they weigh on both art and human experience. She replicates these effects and in doing so provides examples of poor images, that is images that are multiply circulated and in constant processes of mutation and degradation. Through these *poor* images, one can see not only an image of the style and status of contemporary art but also a model of the manifest image of human subjectivity in the *age of dispersion*. To conclude, here are three consequences of this.

First, the *poor* image has characteristics particular to contemporary 'Reality Effects' as Barthes called them. For example, consider the debate around the HD presentation of Peter Jackson's *The Hobbit*. Jackson shot the film in High Frame Rate (HFR), at 48 (rather than 24) frames a second. Whilst this produced a higher definition and smoother image, this had the paradoxical effect of making it look less filmic and thus feel and seem less real. Audiences used to seeing the 'motion blur' and irresolution of traditional cinema interpreted the HD film as unsatisfactory. As film critic Peter Bradshaw observed:

> it looks uncomfortably like telly, albeit telly shot with impossibly high production values and in immersive 3D. Before you grow accustomed to this, it feels as if there has been a terrible mistake in the projection room and they are showing us the video location report from the DVD "making of" featurette, rather than the actual film.[19]

The *poor* image, such as one that exhibits motion blur, can be a satisfactory one; it is a familiar one; it is one in which we can see the circumstances of our experience mirrored.

Second the *poor* image, as an instance of remediation, is isomorphic of more general conditions of remediation that underlie global systems in the *Age of Dispersion*. As has been frequently observed, the systems of late capitalism evolve and survive through a process of remediation whereby objects are transformed into commodities. As Shoshana Zuboff has recently observed a contemporary shift in this process of remediation is the shift to Surveillance Capitalism in which there is shift from natural resources as the source of capital to human activity and experience as the product of fiscal remediation:

> The meadows and the forests and the rivers were turned into commodities that could be sold and purchased – real estate and so forth…. On the small scale, we see this happening around us all the time. There are now apps

to let you know where there's a parking space, and you can actually hire people to go and claim the parking space for you. You're taking a public good and bringing it into the market sphere. Surveillance capitalism is comparable to industrial capitalism's annexation of nature but the commodity that it's creating is based on private human experience.[20]

Contemporary art embodies these conditions perfectly because it relies on the market to which it has always remained attached by an umbilical fibre-optic cord of gold. The paradox is real. As Steyerl acknowledges this attachment and the subsequent paradox of art being a site of critique or resistance:

contemporary art is made possible by neoliberal capital plus the internet, biennials, art fairs, parallel pop-up histories, growing income inequality. Let's add asymmetric warfare—as one of the reasons for the vast redistribution of wealth—real estate speculation, tax evasion, money laundering, and deregulated financial markets to this list.[21]

Third, the structure of this paradox is encapsulated in the difficulty of successfully parsing the content of poor images. This is to propose that the image of glitch, lossy content, degradation, irresolution and ambiguity provides a poor manifest image whilst mirroring the conditions of its production. Might this poor image offer a form of resistance to the increasing annexation of subjectivity in the age of dispersion; a 'how not to be seen'? Thus, if contemporary art is underwritten by an understanding of the contemporary conditions of subjectivity, then in defence of the poor image Steyerl gives us a model of action in the face of these conditions. By virtue of this being a poor and weak image, she also offers a tentative model of a means of resisting the hegemonic effects of global infrastructure by refusing to be fully legible to and within it. Steyerl proposes that art might demonstrate a version of political autonomy by virtue of the unclear messages it communicates or the inaccessible spaces it occupies. The questions of this really being the case rather than just academic wishful thinking and, if so, whether this requires the recouping and rehabilitation of the 'autonomous' enlightenment subject in the 21st century remain open and unanswered.

Notes

1 Hito Steyerl, *Duty Free Art: Art in the Age of Planetary Civil War* (London: Verso, 2017) pg. 87.

2 Hito Steyerl, *Duty Free Art: Art in the Age of Planetary Civil War* (London: Verso, 2017) pg. 78.

3 https://www.universe.com/events/van-gogh-dublin-an-immersive-journey-at-the-rds-tickets-1K9WS2.

4 https://vangoghexpo.com/.

5 Keller Easterling, 'Zone: The Spatial Softwares of Extrastatecraft,' *Places Journal* (June, 2012) https://placesjournal.org/article/zone-the-spatial-softwares-of-extrastatecraft/ (accessed, June 2022)

6 Hito Steyerl, *Duty Free Art: Art in the Age of Planetary Civil War* (London: Verso, 2017) pg. 79.

7 Marc Augé, *Non-Places: Introduction to an Anthropology of Supermodernity: An Introduction to Supermodernity* (London: Verso Books, 2009).

8 Hito Steyerl, *Duty Free Art: Art in the Age of Planetary Civil War* (London: Verso, 2017) pg. 78.

9 Hito Steyerl, 'In Defense of the Poor Image,' *E-Flux Journal*, #10 (November 2009) https://www.e-flux.com/journal/10/61362/in-defense-of-the-poor-image/ (accessed, June 2022)

10 Jay David Bolter and Richard Grusin, *Remediation: Understanding New Media* (Cambridge: MIT Press, 1998).

11 Kenneth Goldsmith, *Uncreative Writing* (New York: Columbia University Press, 2011),

12 'So What Exactly Is Conceptual Writing: An Interview with Kenneth Goldsmith by Katharine Elaine Sanders,' *Bomb Magazine* (October 2nd, 2009) https://bombmagazine.org/articles/so-what-exactly-is-conceptual-writing-an-interview-with-kenneth-goldsmith/ (accessed, June 2022)

13 Claire Bishop, 'The Digital Divide: Contemporary Art and New Media,' *Artforum* (September 2012) https://www.artforum.com/print/201207/digital-divide-contemporary-art-and-new-media-31944 (accessed, June 2022)

14 Irvine Welsh, *T2 Trainspotting* (previously published as *Porno*) (London: Penguin, 2002) pg. 88.

15 George Zarkadakis, *In Our Own Image: Will Artificial Intelligence Save or Destroy Us?* (London: Rider Books, 2015).

16 Wilfred Sellars, 'Philosophy and the Scientific Image of Man,' in Robert Colodny (ed.) *Frontiers of Science and Philosophy* (Pittsburgh, PA: University of Pittsburgh Press, 1962) pp. 35–78; pg. 40.

17 Edmund Husserl, trans. Kersten, 'Foundational Investigations of the Phenomenological Origin of the Spatiality of Nature: The Originary Ark, the Earth, Does Not Move,' in Lawlor & Bergo, (eds.) *Husserl at the Limits of Phenomenology* (Evanston: Northwest University Press, 2002), pp. 117 ff.

18 Sean Carroll, *The Big Picture* (London: Oneworld Publications, 2017), pg. 20.

19 Peter Bradshaw, https://www.theguardian.com/film/2012/dec/09/hobbit-an-unexpected-journey-review.

20 Shoshana Zuboff, (Interview) On the Age of Surveillance Capitalism, *Contagious Magazine* (September 16th, 2019) https://www.contagious.com/news-and-views/shoshana-zuboff-on-the-age-of-surveillance-capitalism (accessed, June 2022)

21 Hito Steyerl, *Duty Free Art: Art in the Age of Planetary Civil War* (London: Verso, 2017) pg. 78.

References

Augé, Marc, *Non-Places: Introduction to an Anthropology of Supermodernity: An Introduction to Supermodernity*, London: Verso Books, 2009

Bishop, Claire, 'The Digital Divide: Contemporary Art and New Media', *Artforum* (September 2012) https://www.artforum.com/print/201207/digital-divide-contemporary-art-and-new-media-31944 (accessed, June 2022)

Bolter, Jay David, and Richard Grusin, *Remediation: Understanding New Media*, Cambridge: MIT Press, 1998

Bradshaw, Peter, https://www.theguardian.com/film/2012/dec/09/hobbit-an-unexpected-journey-review (accessed, 20th July 2022)

Carroll, Sean, *The Big Picture*, London: Oneworld Publications, 2017

Easterling, Keller, 'Zone: The Spatial Softwares of Extrastatecraft', *Places Journal* (June, 2012) https://placesjournal.org/article/zone-the-spatial-softwares-of-extrastatecraft/ (accessed, June 2022)

Goldsmith, Kenneth, *Uncreative Writing*, New York: Columbia University Press, 2011

Husserl, Edmund, trans. Fred Kersten & Leonard Lawlor, 'Foundational Investigations of the Phenomenological Origin of the Spatiality of Nature: The Originary Ark, the Earth, Does Not Move,' in Leonard Lawlor & Bettina Bergo (eds.) *Husserl at the Limits of Phenomenology*, Evanston: Northwest University Press, 2002, pp. 117 ff.

Sanders, Katharine Elaine, 'So What Exactly Is Conceptual Writing: An Interview with Kenneth Goldsmith by Katharine Elaine Sanders', *Bomb Magazine* (October 2nd, 2009) https://bombmagazine.org/articles/so-what-exactly-is-conceptual-writing-an-interview-with-kenneth-goldsmith/ (accessed, June 2022)

Sellars, Wilfred, 'Philosophy and the Scientific Image of Man', in Robert Colodny (ed.) *Frontiers of Science and Philosophy* (pp. 35–78), Pittsburgh: University of Pittsburgh Press, 1962

Steyerl Hito, *Duty Free Art: Art in the Age of Planetary Civil War*, London: Verso, 2017

Steyerl, Hito, 'In Defense of the Poor Image', *E-Flux Journal*, #10 (November 2009) https://www.e-flux.com/journal/10/61362/in-defense-of-the-poor-image/ (accessed, June 2022)

Welsh, Irvine, *T2 Trainspotting* (previously published as *Porno*), London: Penguin, 2002

Zarkadakis, George, *In Our Own Image: Will Artificial Intelligence Save or Destroy Us?* London: Rider Books, 2015

Zuboff, Shoshana, '(Interview) On the Age of Surveillance Capitalism', *Contagious Magazine* (September 16th, 2019) https://www.contagious.com/news-and-views/shoshana-zuboff-on-the-age-of-surveillance-capitalism (accessed, June 2022)

7   Envoi

The End of Art, Again

From the outset, it was stated that this book is about art and the humans that make it. Both, I argue, are systemic and dispersed in the *Age of the Dispersion*. This claim was supported by three assumptions: first, that a model of art is based upon a model of subjectivity, that is an understanding of what art is will be dependent on an understanding of what it means to be human; second, that this dependency is framed by technology, and therefore, as technology changes so do the self-images humans have of themselves. And third, therefore, the technology of late-capitalism and the network society correlates to an aesthetics of systemic and dispersed experience. Art and subjectivity, in the *Age of Dispersion*, are still linked by an umbilical cord, but this is not Greenberg's one of gold that yoked the avant-garde and the bourgeoisie through capital during modernity. Instead, it is now the cords of communication and control, the fibre-optic cables and radio waves of systemic operations that gird the planet that keep things networked together.

The aesthetics of the *Age of Dispersion* is an aesthetics of distribution whereby the object of reflection is indeterminate, ungraspable, blurred. Art is now best understood not only as dispersed across different systems but also as taking this dispersed condition as its main subject matter. It is exemplified by what Hito Steyerl calls the *Poor Image*.

In modernity, it was appropriate to define art by its institutional supports, such as plinths, frames or galleries. These offered necessary guarantees of authenticity when the conditions of art were being interrogated, deconstructed, perturbed and complicated. They also framed and directed aesthetic reflection towards a single discreet object, thereby offering the further guarantee of coupling the autonomy of aesthetic experience with works of art.

These guarantees have now been withdrawn. Their redundancy has been demonstrated by the obvious dead ends of the two main bifurcating paths that led out of modernism (in its hegemonic Western and Northern iterations). On the one hand, the formal experiments of medium specificity have lurched on in an unresolvable endgame from Post-Painterly Abstraction in the 1960s to more recent phenomena such as Zombie Formalism. And on the other,

DOI: 10.4324/9781003315322-8

the legacy of Duchamp and the Readymade as it featured in conceptualism seems to lead to the various different interpretations of the End of Art, be that through a gleeful, anything-goes pluralism of mediums and techniques or the dour anti-aesthetics of the linguistic turn and the eclipsing of art by its own philosophy.

The main text operates with full awareness of these withdrawn guarantees. To conclude, I return to two observations that have, to a certain extent, been bracketed since the foreword. Yet, they remain an important subtext of the whole argument.

First, in Robert Smithson and in particular the figure of the site/non-site one finds a model for art in the *Age of Dispersion* because nested within that figure is a way of understanding humans right now. The site/non-site is a manifest image for ourselves at this moment positioned and constituted, only partially, in social and environmental media of communication and control.

Smithson explored material, entropy and affect. The complex dialectics of site/non-site never resolve into a coherent, fixed and stable identity. Instead, they remain contingent, uncertain and dispersed. In doing so, Smithson offers an alternative route away from the dead ends of modernist medium specificity and anti-art that had been mapped out by Greenberg and Duchamp. This route is still concerned with the affective dimension of aesthetic experience but has no need to be preoccupied with the hygienic marshalling of specific mediums.

Perhaps the reason for this alternative trajectory opened up by Smithson is that he was an outlier in the art world of New York. Apart from some short general classes at the Art Students League of New York and the Brooklyn Museum School, he was mostly self-taught and did not undertake the BA or MFA training that would have grounded his work in debates in painting and sculpture on the legacies of European modernism. This is reflected in his art, which does not, in general, concern itself with the double injunction facing artists of coming to terms with either the problems of abstraction in painting or negotiating the legacy of the Readymade and conceptualism. Such a condition is exemplified by Donald Judd. Judd both drew on his training as a painter to continue the fixation on material purity, formal simplicity and aesthetic austerity that had been inherited from Greenberg's narrative of modernism whilst also synthesising this with preoccupations with seriality, anti-expressionism and the effacing of the unique authorial gesture that was informed by the legacy of Duchamp.

Smithson, however, was neither preoccupied by Greenberg or Duchamp and was dismissive of both. In an interview with Moira Roth about Duchamp in 1973, Smithson repeatedly critiqued Duchamp for being reactionary in that he was: 'mechanistic'; not sufficiently dialectical; and suffused with a latent spiritualism in attempting a transfiguration of the commonplace.[1] Greenberg, however, was responsible for 'visual Puritanism'[2] and with an 'orthodox point of view.'³ In dismissing both, Smithson was free to explore a different trajectory for contemporary art framed by questions of entropy, affect, materialisation and dispersion that, I claim here, provide an effective frame for understanding art in the *Age of Dispersion.*

Second, these examples provide another opportunity to proclaim the end of art, again. Arguments for the end of art are older even than the modernism that supposedly caused the eventual demise of art. Hegel was already proclaiming the eclipsing of art by philosophy at the beginning of the 19th century, decades before either the invention of photography or the Salon de Refuse. Since then, every generation seems to produce its own version of the death of art. However, declaring the end of art in the *Age of Dispersion* has a different character. This is because the impetus for it does not come from debates internal to the discourse of art history and practice but rather from my central claim of the interconnection between art and humans. What it means to be human has radically altered even in my own short lifetime. It is now easily imaginable that the not so distant future will be post-human, trans-human or even non-human. Whether there is a need for art in such a future is still open for debate (Figure 7.1).

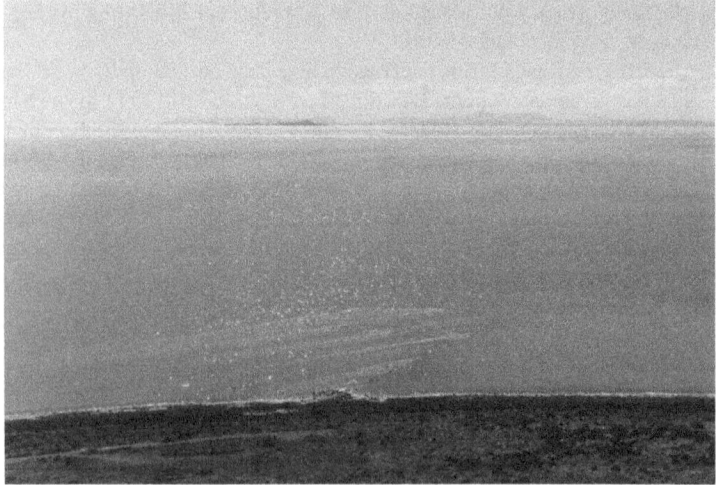

Figure 7.1 Robert Smithson: Spiral Jetty (submerged)

Notes

1 'Robert Smithson on Duchamp: Interview with Moira Roth,' in Jack Flam (ed.) *Robert Smithson: The Collected Writings* (Berkeley: University of California Press, 1996) pp. 310–312.

2 'The Iconography of Desolation,' in Flam (ed.) *Robert Smithson: The Collected Writings* (Berkeley: University of California Press, 1996) pg. 323.

3 'Robert Smithson on Duchamp: Interview with Moira Roth,' in Flam (ed.) *Robert Smithson: The Collected Writings* (Berkeley: University of California Press, 1996) pg. 311.

Reference

'Robert Smithson on Duchamp: Interview with Moira Roth,' in Jack Flam (ed.) *Robert Smithson: The Collected Writings*, Berkley: University of California Press, 1996

Index

Note: *Italic* page numbers refer to figures and page numbers followed by "n" denote endnotes.

92   *Index*

For Product Safety Concerns and Information please contact our EU representative GPSR@taylorandfrancis.com
Taylor & Francis Verlag GmbH, Kaufingerstraße 24, 80331 München, Germany